WORLD ALMANAC® LIBRARY OF THE MIDDLE AGES

Churches and Religion

IN THE MIDDLE AGES

DALE ANDERSON

WORLD ALMANAC® LIBRARY

Please visit our web site at: www.worldalmanaclibrary.com
For a free color catalog describing World Almanac® Library's list of high-quality books
and multimedia programs, call 1-800-848-2928 (USA) or 1-800-387-3178 (Canada).
World Almanac® Library's fax: (414) 332-3567.

Library of Congress Cataloging-in-Publication Data

Anderson, Dale, 1953-
    Churches and religion in the Middle Ages / by Dale Anderson.
        p. cm. — (World Almanac Library of the Middle Ages)
    Includes bibliographical references and index.
    ISBN 0-8368-5892-1 (lib. bdg.)
    ISBN 0-8368-5901-4 (softcover)
    1. Church history—Middle Ages, 600-1500—Juvenile literature. 2. Religions—
History—Juvenile literature. 3. Europe—History—Juvenile literature. I. Title. II. Series.
    BR252.A53   2005
    270.3—dc22   2005043266

First published in 2006 by
World Almanac® Library
A Member of the WRC Media Family of Companies
330 West Olive Street, Suite 100
Milwaukee, WI 53212 USA

Produced by White-Thomson Publishing Ltd.
Editor: Walter Kossmann
Volume editor: Catherine Burch
Designer: Malcolm Walker
Photo researcher: Amy Sparks
World Almanac® Library editorial direction: Valerie J. Weber
World Almanac® Library editor: Jenette Donovan Guntly
World Almanac® Library art direction: Tammy West
World Almanac® Library graphic design: Kami Koenig
World Almanac® Library production: Jessica Morris and Robert Kraus

Photo credits:
AKG-Images pp. 4 (Archives CDA/St.Genes), cover and 5, 34 (British Library), 7, 36 (Schuetze/ Rodemann),
8 (Pirozzi), 22 (Nimatallah), 25 (Gilles Mermet), 29t (Paul M.R. Maeyaert), 31 (Rabatti–Domingie), 33
(Gerhard Ruf), 40 (Volker Kreidler), 42 (Jean-Louis Nou), 9, 32, 37, 38, 39 (AKG Archive); Art Archive pp. 10
(Viking Ship Museum Oslo/Dagli Orti), 12 (Dagli Orti), 14 (Biblioteca Nazionale Marciana Venice/Dagli Orti), 21
(Musée Condé Chantilly/Dagli Orti), 41, 43 (British Library); Bridgeman Art Library pp. 6, 17
(Bridgeman Archive), 11(Bibliothéque Nationale, Paris), 15 (Private Collection), title page and 19
(British Library, London), 23 (St. Paul's Cathedral Library, London), 29b (Peter Willi), 30 (Ken Welsh).

*Cover: A Roman Catholic priest offers **Mass** in this fifteenth-century illuminated manuscript.
Title page: A manuscript illumination shows the conflict in 1076 between King Henry IV of Germany and
Pope Gregory VII about who had the right to name high-ranking Church officials.*

Printed in Canada

1 2 3 4 5 6 7 8 9 09 08 07 06 05

Contents

Words that appear in the glossary are printed in **boldface** type the first time they occur in the text.

Source References on page 45 give bibliographical information on quoted material. See numbers (¹) at the bottom of quotations for their source numbers.

The Middle Ages are the period between ancient and early modern times—the years from about A.D. 500 to 1500. In that time, Europe changed dramatically. The Middle Ages began with the collapse of the **Roman Empire** and with "**barbarian**" tribes invading from the north and east. In the early years of the Middle Ages, western European farmers struggled to survive. This period ended with European merchants eagerly seeking new international markets, European travelers searching for lands and continents unknown to them to explore, European artists creating revolutionary new styles, and European thinkers developing powerful new ideas in religion, government, and philosophy.

What Were the "Middle Ages" Like?

Some people view the period as the "Dark Ages," an era marked by ignorance and brutality. It is true that **medieval** people faced difficult lives marred by hard work, deadly diseases, and dreadful wars, but their lives included more than that.

◄ Cathedrals like this one at Chartres, France, stand as impressive monuments of the Middle Ages.

A HISTORIAN'S VIEW

"A hundred years ago the medieval centuries . . . were widely regarded as 'The Dark Ages.' . . . It was an age whose art was barbaric or '**Gothic**'—a millennium of darkness—a thousand years without a bath. Today . . . scholarship [has] demonstrated clearly that the medieval period was an epoch of immense vitality and profound creativity."
C. Warren Hollister [1]

The Middle Ages were also a time of growing population, developing technology, increasing trade, and fresh ideas. New villages and towns were built; new fields were cleared; and, with the help of new tools like the wheeled iron plow, farms produced more food. **Caravans** brought silks and spices from faraway lands in Asia. New sports and games, such as soccer, golf, chess, and playing cards, became popular. Musicians, singers, acrobats, and dancers entertained crowds at fairs and festivals. Traveling troupes performed plays that mixed humor with moral messages for anyone who would stop and listen.

Religion, education, and government all changed. Christianity spread throughout Europe and became more powerful. Another major faith—Islam—was born and carried into Europe from the Middle East. New schools and universities trained young men as scholars or

◀ This page from an illustrated book shows Roman Catholic priests celebrating **Mass**, one of the most sacred rituals of the Roman Catholic Church.

for careers in the Church, medicine, and the law. Medieval rulers, judges, and ordinary citizens created **parliaments**, jury trials, and the common law. These changes in the fabric of society still shape our world today.

Historians divide the entire period into two parts. In the early Middle Ages, from about A.D. 500 to 1000, Europe adjusted to the changes caused by the fall of the Roman Empire and the formation of new kingdoms by **Germanic** peoples. In these years, the Christian Church took form and Europeans withstood new invasions. In the late Middle Ages, from about 1000 to 1500, medieval life and culture matured. This period saw population growth and economic expansion, the rise of towns and universities, the building of great cathedrals and mosques, and the launching of the **Crusades**.

Religion in the Middle Ages

Most Europeans in the Middle Ages were Roman Catholics, but some belonged to the Eastern

Orthodox Church, to Judaism, or to Islam. Whatever the faith, religion stood at the center of society.

Religion shaped people's lives. People worked every day except for the days they took off once a week to worship and for yearly holidays— "holy days"—set aside for religious celebrations. When people had problems, felt ill, or wished to marry, they turned to their priest, rabbi, or mullah for help.

Religion and government were also closely connected. Islamic, Eastern Orthodox, and Roman Catholic rulers all issued laws in the name of their God.

Finally, religion linked people from different areas. Roman Catholicism united people across much of Europe. People did not see themselves as Europeans but as part of "Christendom"—an area defined by a shared faith. Jews, Muslims, and Eastern Orthodox Christians also felt they belonged to a community of believers—no matter where they lived.

forming the Christian Church

In the Middle Ages, the Roman Catholic Church dominated European culture and society. Grand cathedrals towered above cities, and Church officials controlled great wealth and power. Priests brought the teachings of the Church to nearly every small village. Yet, the Church began as just a small band of believers in an obscure corner of the Roman Empire, the area of today's Israel and the West Bank.

The Beginnings of Christianity

Christianity is based on the teachings of Jesus, a Jew who lived in the first century A.D. He taught that people should love one another and forgive their enemies. Those who believed in God would be given eternal happiness in heaven after they died. About A.D. 30, Jesus was arrested and accused of treason. The Roman governor of the area had him executed by crucifying him, or nailing him to a cross.

Jesus' followers believed that he was God in human form and that he had saved them by dying on the cross. They believed that Jesus' sacrifice won forgiveness of their sins and eternal life after death.

Why Is It Called "Christianity"?

Jesus' followers believed he was the Messiah. According to Jewish belief, God would send the Messiah to restore the Jewish kingdom and bring about a new age of peace and prosperity. Thus Jesus was called *Christos*, or *Christ*– Greek for "Messiah." Christians, then, are believers in Christ.

Belief in Jesus Spreads

After Jesus' death, his followers carried on his teaching. Early on, a **convert** named Paul began preaching the faith not just to Jews but also to non-Jews. Gradually the faith spread throughout the Roman Empire.

As the religion grew, some Roman officials saw Christians as a problem. Roman law required people to support the official religion. That religion included belief in many gods, one of whom was the Roman emperor. Christians refused to worship these gods, and as a result, some Roman officials **persecuted** them. They arrested believers and even killed some. Despite these attacks, the faith continued to spread.

◄ This wall painting from the mid-third century shows a shepherd with his sheep. Early Christians believed that Jesus cared for all believers just as a shepherd cares for his sheep.

Defining the Faith

In the fourth century A.D., Christianity changed dramatically. When the general Constantine became the Roman emperor, he ended all persecution of Christians and declared them free to worship. The emperor also gave money to build churches and said church officials did not have to pay taxes. In A.D. 380, the Emperor Theodosius went further. He made Christianity the official religion of the Roman Empire.

As Christianity grew, leaders began to build the institution that eventually became the Roman Catholic Church. One step was to decide which writings would be considered sacred, and these came to form the Christian Bible. Four books—called the Gospels—told the story of Jesus and

▲ This church, built in the sixth century in Ravenna, Italy, differs from typical medieval Christian churches. Instead of being built in the shape of a cross, as were most churches of that time, this church has eight sides.

included words he had spoken. Most of these books were written in the first few decades after Jesus' death.

Another important step was to define the core set of ideas that would be official Christian beliefs. Christians living in different areas sometimes had different beliefs. One key difference concerned the nature of Jesus. Most Christians believed that Christ was God in human form. A Christian leader named Arius disagreed. He preached that Jesus was not of the same nature as God, and many Christians adopted this view. This disagreement deeply divided early Christians. In A.D. 325, Constantine ordered a council of Christian leaders to meet in Nicaea, an ancient city in what is now Turkey. This council decided that Arius's teachings were **heresy**.

Organizing the Church

The early Church leaders began to set up an organization. At first, there were no official priests. Elders, who were respected members of each group of worshipers, oversaw services. Eventually, Christians developed two kinds of **clergy**: secular clergy and regular clergy. Priests belonged to the secular clergy. They worked in the world, holding services at local churches and meeting the spiritual needs of ordinary people. Regular clergy were monks who spent their days in work and prayer in communities called **monasteries**.

The position of an elder developed into the office of a bishop. Bishops played key roles in building the Church. They promoted the spread of Christianity in the areas where they worked. They also joined together to strengthen the growing Church. Bishops attended the council at Nicaea and other councils. Some wrote important books explaining what it meant to be a Christian. Three of these writers—Augustine, Jerome, and Ambrose—influenced the Church throughout the Middle Ages. They and other early figures came to be called "Church Fathers."

A few bishops were thought to have the highest status. They included the bishop of Constantinople, the capital of the Roman Empire, and the bishop of Rome. The high place of Rome's bishop stemmed from tradition. Jesus had told his **apostle** Peter that Peter would be the "rock" on which the Church would be built. Since Peter was the first bishop of Rome, later bishops there said they inherited this special authority. Eventually, the bishop of Rome came to be called the pope.

Expansion and Division

While the majority of people in the Roman Empire were Christians, most people living outside it were not. Some were still **pagans**. Many

◀ One task monks performed in their monasteries was to copy books. Some books had pages, like this one from Ireland in the eighth century, decorated with elaborate and colorful illustrations.

others had adopted Arius's, or Arian, beliefs, not those approved at the Council of Nicaea. Throughout the next few hundred years, Christian leaders devoted much attention to converting the pagans and Arians. By the late tenth century, though, most of Europe—from Ireland to Italy and from Spain to Serbia—was Christian.

While Christianity was spreading, divisions grew between Christians in western Europe and those in eastern Europe. One sore point was the issue of authority. The pope, Leo IX, claimed to be the highest authority in the Church. However, the senior bishop in Constantinople—the patriarch, Michael Cerularius—said his authority was equal. There were differences in beliefs and practices as well.

These disputes led to a break between the two areas in 1054. That year, representatives of the pope, Leo IX, declared that the patriarch Michael Cerularius and all who followed him were **excommunicated**. The patriarch, in turn, excommunicated the pope. From that point, the Christian Church in the west became known as the Roman Catholic Church. The Church in the east became known as the Eastern Orthodox Church.

Adapting the Church to the People

To gain support among pagans, the Church transformed pagan practices. For instance, the Church turned pagan religious festivals into Christian holidays. The people of Britain and Ireland believed that spirits of the dead walked the Earth on November 1. They followed various rituals to protect themselves from those spirits, including wearing masks and disguises. Hoping to suppress this belief, Pope Gregory IV made November 1 All Saints' Day, a religious holiday. The switch worked—but only partly. Christian converts in the British Isles did honor the **saints** but also kept the older tradition alive. They simply shifted it to the day before, which is now celebrated as Halloween.

► This painting shows Augustine blessing the person who paid for the painting while an angel watches. This work from the early fifteenth century shows how respected Augustine remained nearly one thousand years after his death.

CHAPTER 2

Problems and Reform

By the year 1000, the Christian Church was a mature institution. It was also rebounding from attacks by Muslims, Magyars, and Vikings that had damaged or destroyed some churches and monasteries. The next two hundred years saw a new surge of religious feeling among Church leaders and ordinary people. This new feeling brought important changes to the Church.

The Church in 1000

The eighth, ninth, and tenth centuries had brought three waves of invasion to Europe. Muslims, who are followers of Islam, had swept up from North Africa to capture Sicily, southern Italy, and much of Spain. A group called the Magyars had moved into central Europe, attacking towns and villages. They finally settled in what is now Hungary, and they converted to Catholicism. Vikings had stormed down from the north to raid towns and cities. These raiders also plundered monasteries and churches, taking valuable objects and sometimes burning what they left. Like the Germanic peoples before them, the Vikings had settled down by the tenth century and set up new kingdoms. They also joined the Christian Church.

Still, the raids had hurt the Church. Some monasteries had been destroyed, and others had lost members. Partly as a result of the raids, monasteries passed into the control of local nobles, and this weakened them. Some nobles kept the rent money monasteries were supposed to receive for their church lands. Most of the nobles had little interest in forcing the monks to live according to monastic rule. The monasteries continued to exist, but they were no longer centers of prayer and worship. A council of French bishops complained that monks were "forgetful of their profession [and] occupied in worldly business."

> ## GRIEF ABOUT VIKING ATTACKS
>
> *"Behold the Church of St. Cuthbert spattered with the blood of the priests of God, despoiled of all its ornaments; a place more venerable than all in Britain is given as a prey to pagan peoples. . . . What should be expected for other places, when the divine judgment has not spared this holy place?"*
> **Alcuin of York, letter** [2]

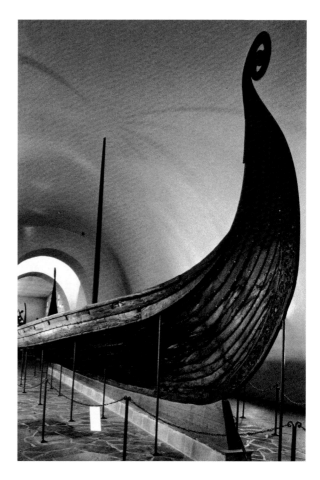

▶ This preserved Viking longship is similar to those used by early Vikings to cross the North Sea to raid monasteries in other parts of Europe.

The Rise of Religious Feeling

The raids and violence produced fears that the Second Coming of Christ was near. That event was supposed to lead to the end of the world and the Day of Judgment. On that day, Jesus would return to Earth and decide the fate of every human. Believers whose sins were forgiven would be saved and allowed to live forever in heaven. Those found too sinful would be condemned to live forever in hell. Fear of this

▲ This painting shows pilgrims near the Church of the Holy Sepulcher in Jerusalem. The church is thought to be built on the site where Jesus' tomb had been.

coming event grew throughout the tenth century. Many people were certain that the ending of the first millennium after Christ would see the end of the world. When it did not, there was widespread relief.

Thinking about the Second Coming led to a rise in religious fervor across Europe. These

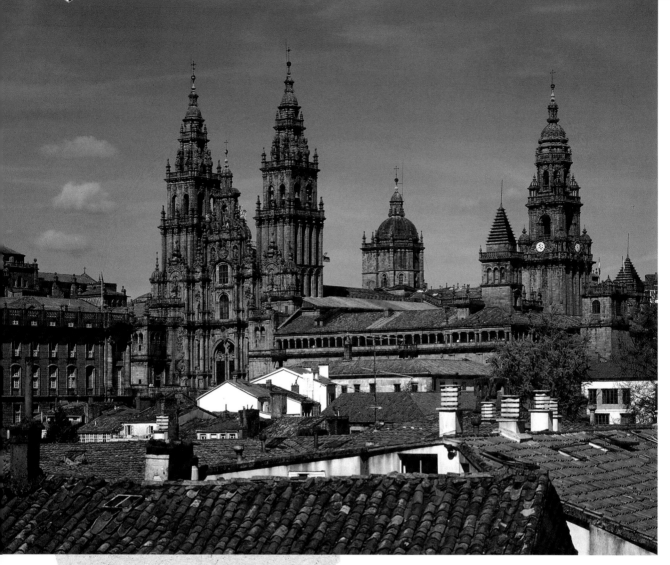

Pilgrimage Sites

Rome and Jerusalem drew pilgrims throughout the Middle Ages. Other sites saw their popularity rise and fall with time. Canterbury, England, held the bones of Thomas Becket, an archbishop who had been murdered and was then made a saint. When word spread that visiting his tomb cured sickness, pilgrims began flocking there, but after just a few years, the site lost its popularity. Santiago de Compostela in Spain remained popular throughout the Middle Ages. Even today, some people take a walking stick and shell, symbols of that pilgrimage, and follow the old route to the cathedral in that city.

▲ Santiago de Compostela, Spain, supposedly the burial place of Saint James's bones, is still the destination of pilgrimages by devout Christians.

deeper feelings of devotion to God continued even after the Second Coming did not happen.

One sign of this growing religious feeling was a rise in the number of people going on **pilgrimages**. The main destinations of these pilgrims were the sites Christians saw as holy. The chief goal was the **Holy Land** and especially Jerusalem, where Jesus had spent his last days. Rome was another important destination for pilgrims, as it held the tombs of Peter and Paul.

PLEDGE FOR PEACE

"No Christian shall kill another Christian, for whoever kills a Christian undoubtedly sheds the blood of Christ."
Council of Narbonne, 1054 [3]

Another popular city was Santiago de Compostela in the northwest corner of Spain. Santiago is Spanish for Saint James, one of Jesus' apostles. In 813, a tomb was discovered near the Spanish city. When miracles began to occur, the local bishop decided that the tomb held the bones of Saint James. Soon people began taking the difficult trek over hard mountain roads to reach this now holy city.

Another sign of renewed religious feeling was the growing popularity of **relics**. Many churches and monasteries claimed to have the bones of a

the Role of Saints

Early in the Church's history, some people were recognized as especially holy figures who should be honored, and they came to be called saints. They included Jesus' twelve faithful apostles, Paul, and those **martyred** during the Roman persecutions. In the tenth century, the Church named certain requirements for a person to achieve sainthood. They included leading a moral life and having two miracles credited to him or her.

Saints are honored on a particular date, or feast day. Some saints are considered the patron saints of particular groups. Saint Agnes is the patron of girls, Saint Nicholas of sailors, and Saint Patrick of Ireland. In the Middle Ages, cities and countries staged major festivals on the feast days of their patron saints.

Catholics believe that saints can intervene with God to help them. People also pray to their favorite saint for guidance, or help, when they face a problem.

saint or objects from Jesus' life, such as a piece of the cross. The cathedral at Chartres, in northern France, was supposed to hold a piece of the clothing Mary wore when Jesus was born. Pilgrims traveled far to make offerings to these relics. That money went into the treasury of the church or monastery holding the relic.

Seeking a Purer Life and Peace

Some Christians showed their religious feeling by separating themselves from society and living as hermits. They aimed to live a simple, more spiritual life, as the apostles had lived. Some of these people denied themselves all physical comforts and lived completely alone. Others gave up comfort but did not wish to be alone. They settled down with a group of friends, and all devoted themselves to prayer together.

Some people chose to become **anchorites**. These were people who agreed to have themselves sealed in small rooms with only a small window. Once inside, they devoted themselves to prayer and depended on the community to provide food and clothing. A large percentage of these anchorites were women. Some chose this course to avoid marriages that had been arranged for them against their wishes.

The upsurge in religious feeling led to a peace movement. Since Christ's message had been peace, some Christians worked to reduce war and its ill effects. A Church council in France urged that innocent people and clergy be spared harm when two armies fought. Another council went further, declaring that people who fought wars should be excommunicated. As the movement gained support, people came together to pledge that they would not fight.

A related idea was called the Truce of God. People urged that armies refrain from fighting on Sundays and holy days. Later in the eleventh century, the truce period stretched from Wednesday to Monday. Many rulers agreed to the truce—though they often ignored it when

▲ This illustration from the thirteenth century shows hermits dressed in plain clothing. These religious men gave up most comforts and tried to live simple, pure lives.

convenient. Even though it was not always followed, the peace movement showed a growing desire for more order and stability.

Reform in the Church

The renewed religious spirit swept the Church as well. New leaders aimed to reform the Church and its practices. Leading this movement were several popes, starting with Leo IX. Made pope in 1049, he gathered about him talented monks who were dedicated, like him, to ending abuses

Devotion to Mary

Mary—the mother of Jesus—had always been an important figure among Christians as one of the first people to believe in his mission. The Ave Maria (Hail Mary), a prayer to her, first came into use in the sixth century. In the twelfth century, devotion to Mary gained new popularity. Churches, cathedrals, and monasteries were dedicated to her. Artists sculpted and painted images of her. She was given new titles, including "Queen of Heaven." Preachers said that she would intervene on behalf of people with God. That might explain why she was so popular. Mary remains an important figure in the Roman Catholic Church today.

Electing the Pope

The reformers tried to end outside influence on the Church by changing how the pope was chosen. Originally there were no actual rules for choosing the pope. For centuries, powerful Roman families made the choice, although sometimes they were swayed to pick a particular candidate by the Roman mob or powerful rulers. In 1059, Pope Nicholas II decreed that only cardinals—then a group of bishops who headed particular churches near Rome—had the authority to elect the pope. The new rule was not always applied, however. The reformer Gregory VII was made pope, ironically, by a Roman crowd. Eventually, though, the choice was left to the cardinals alone.

▶ Before he became pope, Gregory VII worked as an administrator of papal finances for several earlier popes. He was particularly interested in ending corruption in the Church.

in the Church and increasing the power of the **papacy**. One of those monks became pope himself in 1073, taking the name Gregory VII.

One reform was to stop priests from marrying. Until then, many parish priests and some bishops had wives. The reformers believed that the clergy needed to focus on caring for the spiritual needs of people. That meant they should not marry. Priests and bishops across Europe

protested, and the reform took a long time to take hold. By about 1200, though, married priests were rare.

The reformers took aim at another practice. They wanted to end the custom of buying positions in the clergy, called **simony**. Popes Leo IX and Gregory VII campaigned vigorously against this abuse. While they did not manage to eliminate simony, the practice did become less common.

Building the Papacy

The reformers wanted to increase the power of the papacy. Several popes began to organize Church rules into a system called canon law. Learned men studied Church councils and decrees made by earlier popes. They outlined rules on each problem that the Church faced or each Church teaching. Sometimes it was found that past decrees disagreed with each other, but any questions that still remained were settled by the pope making a final decision. Building the system of canon law helped put more power in the pope's hands.

As the papacy grew stronger, it needed more people to work for it. Popes hired lawyers to work on building canon law. They hired clerks to send messages to Church officials in other lands. To help run this larger papacy, the reformers changed the role of the cardinals. In the eighth century, the cardinals had started helping the popes by doing administrative work. Over time, cardinals were placed in charge of the different departments in the Church's government.

By about 1200, the papacy was a very powerful institution. Historians call it "the papal monarchy" because the pope ruled the Roman Catholic Church as a king ruled a nation.

The Local Church

The pope, of course, was distant from the majority of Christians. Since most people lived in the countryside, they also had little contact with the bishops, who often lived in cities. A parish priest usually represented the Christian Church to most people and instructed and preached to these people. In the early Middle Ages, priests were very similar to the people of their parish. Many were married, and many did not have very much education. By the thirteenth century, the situation was very different. By and large, Church reformers had ceased to allow married priests. The Church made sure that priests were better educated. Priests even began to look different

to their **parishioners**. In 1215, a Church council ruled that priests had to wear special clothing.

Priests taught the basic beliefs of the Church to the people of the parish. They led church services and conducted Mass. Priests also heard confessions, when parishioners told them what sins they had committed, and in reply, priests told people what **penance** they had to perform to have their sins forgiven. In 1215, the Fourth Lateran Council made confessing a central part of the Roman Catholic faith for all members of the Church. At least once each year, the council said, each parishioner must confess his or her sins to the parish priest and take part in Easter Mass. Any Catholic who failed to do this could be excluded from the Church.

Finally, the priests were present for three important stages in people's lives. They **baptized** children into the Church, they married couples, and they gave the last rites to the dying.

Parishioners were supposed to give one-tenth of their income, called a tithe, to the local church. That money provided the priest's income. Some priests were in charge of more than one parish. Since they could not be at all of them at the same time, they put some parishes in the hands of another priest called a vicar. Vicars had the right to only one-third of the parish income. The rest went to the chief priest. As a result, most vicars were poor and led difficult lives.

With their many responsibilities, priests needed help. Other members of the clergy worked beneath them to provide that help. Those who served as deacons did some of the readings from the Bible during Mass. If someone had enough learning, he could work as a clerk and help the priest with keeping records and writing letters.

▶ The tower of a church in southern England rises above the parish burial ground. Most Catholics worshiped in village churches like this one, not in the great cathedrals found in cities.

CHAPTER 3

Church and State

opes were the spiritual leaders of the Catholic world. They also controlled some lands in Italy, just as a prince or king would. These two areas of responsibility—the Church and the State—sometimes led to conflicts between popes and rulers. Some popes claimed that, as God's representatives, they had supreme power on Earth—and thus kings and emperors had to obey them. Some popes clashed with rulers in the effort to protect the lands held by the papacy.

Pope and Ruler

Popes and rulers often confronted a central question: Which of them had the greater authority? Examples from the Roman Empire were confusing. Emperor Constantine had called the Council of Nicaea in A.D. 325, suggesting he had greater authority. On the other hand, he did not interfere in the council's decisions and agreed to follow them. In the fifth century, Pope Gelasius I recognized a split between political and religious power. He said, however, that rulers should obey the Church on matters involving religion.

Two popes, Leo III and Stephen II, took steps that seemed to place their authority—which came from God—higher than that of a ruler. In ancient Israel, holy men poured oil on the head of a king when he was crowned. This act symbolized that the king owed his kingship to God. In 754 and 800, this act was performed when crowning Pepin the Short as king of the Franks and Charlemagne as emperor of Rome. In doing so, the popes showed all Christians that Pepin and Charlemagne received the right to rule from them.

Pope Gregory VII carried the claim of higher authority the furthest. He argued that the pope "is to be judged by no one," but that the pope "may depose emperors." In fact, if the pope believed that a ruler was unjust, he could excuse that country's subjects from any need to obey him. These claims of supremacy led directly to a conflict with King Henry IV of Germany.

The Clash Begins

The dispute between the popes and rulers centered on **lay investiture**, which is the right of a ruler to appoint people to high-level positions in the Church without the pope's approval. King Henry IV of Germany wanted to keep that right, and Pope Gregory VII wanted to take it away. Henry wanted to be able to appoint high Church officials because they owed a king certain duties, such as sending him soldiers when he requested. He wanted to place friends in these offices, so he could count on them to supply those soldiers.

SEPARATION OF CHURCH AND STATE

"There are two powers by which this world is chiefly ruled, august emperor: the sacred authority of the [popes] and the royal power. . . . You know that, even though you surpass the human race in dignity, nevertheless you piously bow your head to those who have charge of divine affairs and . . . in the order of religion, you ought to submit yourself to them rather than rule."
Pope Gelasius I, letter to Emperor Anastasius I [4]

▶ These scenes show the end of the investiture conflict between King Henry IV and Pope Gregory VII. In the top panel, Henry sits at his table with soldiers outside. In the bottom, his troops confront the pope, whose death is shown in the lower right.

solacıū qdᵭ ıñ tuıf aurıb; lıceat an
ktaucı̈ cumulū deplozare S; unde
sumet̄ exordıū. Na dıcendı parıt
ınopıā maᵗıa copıofa & exubant.
& qⁱ uıfı tēpe ñᵒ malıcıa extreuı
fet ad ſtⁱmū. fıdē extredıt. Publıcā
angufꞇaſ an domeſꞇıcaſ deploza
boꝛꝰ S; gⁱaleſ muııꝺ agnouıt. ſua

K ınſpato & ıñ tꝛıſꞇıū ıñ
dı gᵗa �procıautte ııı ıꝓ
ınnotuıt; qdᵭ ad uoſ e
rat lator ꝓſencıū tꝛıſꞇı
tur. Gaucıſuf g̃ dıuıuı
& mıuııſꞇꝛacā occaſıonē ſꞇbendı ad
amıcū ea gᵗanᵗ arrıpuı; arbıtꝛıuſ

The Donation of Constantine

To support their claims of authority, popes pointed to a document called "The Donation of Constantine." The paper was supposedly written by the ancient Roman emperor back in the fourth century. In it, Constantine gave the pope authority over all lands in the western part of the empire. The document was a complete fake created in the eighth century. Nevertheless, popes used it for centuries to justify the idea that rulers had to answer to them. In the fifteenth century, an Italian scholar proved it to be false.

► Knights carry out the wishes of King Henry II of England and kill his onetime friend Thomas Becket, the archbishop of Canterbury. The Church moved quickly after Becket's death to name him a saint.

emperor of the Holy Roman Empire. The Holy Roman Empire was an area made up mostly of modern Germany but also containing parts of Italy. Gregory died in exile a few years later.

Settling the Question

Meanwhile, the issue of lay investiture remained unsettled. In 1122, a new pope, Callistus II, and a new emperor, Henry V, reached an agreement. The pope would fill all Church offices, though the emperor could be present when the selection was made and could step in when there was a dispute. In return, bishops would show their allegiance to the emperor for the lands they held in his name.

However, other rulers were still unwilling to give up the right to fill Church offices. King John of England refused to accept an archbishop named by Pope Innocent III. The pope excommunicated him, and King John was forced to back down. He could not march on Rome, as Henry IV of Germany had done, for it was too far from England. Like Henry, John faced rebellious nobles and had little political support at home.

Even when kings did control appointments to Church offices, their choices could backfire. King Henry II of England named his close friend and adviser Thomas Becket as archbishop of Canterbury. Some years later, Becket was faced with a difficult decision in which he had to choose whether to help the Church or the king. When Becket chose the option better for the Church, an exasperated Henry is said to have called out, "Will no one of my men rid me of this contemptuous, low-born priest?" Four knights promptly rode to Canterbury and murdered Becket. To remove the stain of his role in the murder, Henry had to travel to Canterbury and humble himself by doing public penance.

To Pope Gregory, lay investiture contradicted the pope's supreme authority over Church officials and all rulers. Early in 1075, Gregory convinced a Roman Catholic Church council to declare that lay investiture was wrong and that any ruler who carried it out would be punished. Some time later, Henry defied the ruling by naming a new archbishop. The angry pope quickly excommunicated the king and removed Henry from his kingship. Henry called his own Church council. That group, following his orders, excommunicated the pope.

Henry's position was difficult, and German nobles sided with the pope. If the king were weakened, they thought, they would become stronger. Without their support, Henry had to beg forgiveness. He traveled to a castle in northern Italy where Gregory was staying. With wife and child in hand, the king stood in the snow for three days while Gregory figured out what to do. Finally, the pope lifted his order against the king.

Henry then returned to Germany only to find his nobles in revolt. Once Henry had defeated them, he led his army south to Rome. Unable to gather enough support, Gregory had to flee. Henry took the city and put a rival pope in office. That pope cooperated by naming Henry as

Du martyre de lui

Popes and Politics

Popes also took part in power politics. In the eighth century, Pepin the Short, king of the Franks, gave the papacy control over a wide belt of land in central Italy, including Rome. This area came to be called the Papal States. From then on, popes were not just the heads of the Roman Catholic Church but also rulers, just like any king. To protect their hold on this land, popes became deeply involved in the politics of Europe. They supported rulers who helped secure their control of the Papal States and opposed those who threatened that control.

Sometimes their strong interest in the Papal States forced them to change sides. In the 1040s and 1050s, large numbers of **Norman** knights came to southern Italy and set up their own kingdom there. At first the popes opposed the Normans, but as the Normans gained success, Pope Nicholas II switched positions. He made a deal with the Norman leader Robert Guiscard. Later, when Guiscard seemed to threaten the Papal States, Pope Gregory VII turned against him. Guiscard won the pope back during the investiture conflict, though. When Henry IV marched toward Rome, Guiscard sent soldiers to defend the pope.

Popes also clashed with rulers about other issues involving control of the Roman Catholic Church. In the late thirteenth century, the kings of England and France were both desperate for money to pay for a war they were fighting against each other. Both decided to force Church officials to pay taxes, which broke tradition. When Pope Boniface VIII ordered the clergy not to pay, King Philip IV of France blocked the flow of Church income from his country to Rome. The pope had to give in.

Popes used their Church powers to help—or hinder—political allies. The Roman Catholic Church did not allow divorce, but sometimes kings wanted to change wives. The pope might agree to annul the marriage of a friendly king but refuse it to rulers who opposed him.

Popes also used their power to help their own families advance. They could give brothers and cousins high-level Church offices or put them in charge of lands that the papacy controlled.

▶ Boniface VIII, pope from 1294 to 1303, issued a strong declaration of the pope's powers. He wrote, "It is altogether necessary for the salvation of every human creature [even rulers] to be subject to" the pope.

▶ This document is an indulgence granted by the bishop of London around 1120. The bishop's seal at the top shows it was an official document.

Purgatory and Indulgences

Early in the Church's history, a belief arose in a third destination for the dead, in addition to heaven for the saved and hell for those not saved. The third location came to be called purgatory. In purgatory, people who had committed sins but not fully done penance for them could stay until that penance was complete. They, too, could then reach heaven. By praying and doing good works, the living could reduce the time their departed loved ones spent in purgatory. Late in the Middle Ages, the Roman Catholic Church gave people a new way to reduce a soul's time in purgatory. They could buy papers called indulgences. In the early sixteenth century, outrage over that practice led to the Protestant Reformation. That movement broke apart the Roman Catholic Church and eventually led to the rise of Protestantism, Anglicanism, and other religious groups.

The Power and the Glory

By 1200, the Roman Catholic Church was a wealthy institution. Money flowed into the Church treasury from offerings made at churches. The income from the large estates linked to monasteries or controlled by bishops also provided wealth.

The funds were used in many different ways. The Church ran hospitals and orphanages and provided aid to the poor. The Church also bought relics to attract the faithful. Bishops ordered paintings, sculptures, and items made of gold, silver, or precious stones to decorate their cathedrals and illustrate God's glory. Some less-religious Church officials used some of the money to support their lives of luxury and comfort.

CHAPTER 4

Crusades, Cathedrals, and Schools

 hile popes were changing the Church and increasing their own power, the Roman Catholic Church was flexing its muscles. Kings and popes launched crusades—or holy wars—against Muslims. Christians expressed their devotion to God by building magnificent new churches. Brilliant thinkers worked to show how rational thinking could be joined with religious faith.

The Reconquista

In the eighth century, Muslims had conquered much of modern Spain and Portugal. Christian kings, holed up in the north, were determined to win back the land. They launched the movement called the Reconquista, or reconquest.

By A.D.1000, there were five key Christian kingdoms in the **Iberian** peninsula: León, Navarre, Aragon, Castile, and Portugal. The kings of these areas often fought the Muslims. In the eleventh century, León and Castile were joined together and made major gains on Muslim lands. After 1200, Muslim control shrank further, although Muslims kept a toehold in the south. In 1249, the king of Portugal, Alfonso III, reconquered the last part of Portugal from the Muslims. In the late fifteenth century, Isabella of Castile and Ferdinand of Aragon married, thus uniting their major Christian kingdoms. They defeated the last Muslim kingdom in 1492.

The Reconquista brought more people into the Christian Church. Some were Christians who had lived in Muslim lands, and some were Muslims. Christian rulers sometimes allowed these Muslims to continue practicing their faith. Sometimes, though, Muslims were forced to convert or to leave the country. Jews who had lived in Muslim areas were left alone for many decades. Soon after the Reconquista was completed, however, all Jews were ordered to leave Spain unless they converted.

The Reconquista had far-reaching effects. For a long time, scholars in Muslim lands had studied the writings of ancient Greek scientists and philosophers. These works had not been known in western Europe since the end of the Roman Empire. When Christian armies took Muslim cities, these ancient works came into Christian hands. Spanish scholars translated them into Latin and shipped the books to other countries across Europe.

Spain's Hero—El Cid

The Spanish military leader Rodrigo Díaz de Vivar was more commonly known as "El Cid," from the Arabic for "lord." El Cid gained early fame by helping the Christian king of Castile defeat the Muslim king of Zaragoza. Later, however, he angered a key ally of Castile's new king, and the king exiled him. El Cid spent the next ten years fighting for the Muslims, sometimes defeating Christian armies. In 1094, he conquered the city of Valencia for himself. Soon after his death, a long poem emerged. It portrayed El Cid as a warrior of skill, a man of honor, and a hero of the Reconquista. That—and not the more complex reality—is how many Spanish remember him.

▶ In this sculpture from a Spanish church, the Muslim king of Granada gives the keys of the kingdom to Queen Isabella and King Ferdinand. This surrender marked the completion of the Christian reconquest.

Taking Southern Italy for the Faith

The Muslims had also captured Sicily and southern Italy in the ninth century. There, as in Spain, Christians were left alone, though some did convert. Muslim rule brought prosperity, making the region attractive to others. In the 1060s, Normans came to the area determined to conquer it. Their success in 1091 made Christianity the main faith there. The Normans quickly set up monasteries and built churches. Here, as in Spain, Muslim scholarship was translated into Latin, bringing new knowledge.

Still, large numbers of Muslims remained, and the Normans made no effort to force them to convert. Christians and Muslims lived in relative peace for many decades. Over time, however, Christians made life difficult for Muslims, and the followers of Islam left Italy.

Holy War

Between 1095 and 1270, Catholic Europe launched a series of military expeditions called Crusades. Their goal was to take the Holy Land out of Muslim hands. The impetus for the Crusades came from a number of factors. For some years, Muslim armies had been making the journeys of pilgrims to Jerusalem more difficult. Muslim armies had threatened the **Byzantine Empire**, and the emperor asked Urban II for aid. The fighting in Spain and Sicily had created the idea that war against Muslims was just.

Pope Urban II called for the First Crusade in 1095, appealing to Christian knights to march east. The Roman Catholic Church offered to remove all sins of all those who fought. Thousands responded, and a force was on the move by late 1096. The next year, the crusaders reached Asia Minor—what is now Turkey—and defeated a Muslim army at Dorylaeum with overwhelming numbers. In 1098 they won the battle of Antioch and captured several cities in present-day Syria and Israel, including Aleppo and Edessa. Finally, in 1099, they took Jerusalem and killed huge numbers of people, including women and children, in a bloody massacre.

THE MASSACRE IN JERUSALEM

"After [entering Jerusalem] our men rushed round the whole city, seizing gold and silver, horses and mules, and houses full of all sorts of goods, and they all came rejoicing and weeping from excess of gladness to worship at the Sepulcher of our Savior Jesus. . . . Next morning they . . . attacked the [Muslims], both men and women, cutting off their heads with drawn swords. . . . No one has ever seen or heard of such a slaughter . . . and no one save God alone knows how many there were."
Anonymous, *Gesta Francorum*, c. 1100 [5]

The crusaders divided the conquered area into sections ruled by nobles who had joined the fight. These were called the Crusader States. Within a few years, the crusaders extended their control in the area by taking some coastal cities.

Later Crusades

In the next few decades, Muslim armies retook Edessa and some of the other areas they had lost to the Christians. In the 1140s, Christians launched the Second Crusade. This failed when King Louis VII of France was unable to capture Damascus (now the capital of Syria). A powerful Muslim leader, Saladin, arose in Egypt and began retaking parts of the Holy Land. In 1187, his forces defeated a Christian army at Hattin, which enabled the Muslims to recapture Jerusalem.

As a result, the Third Crusade began in 1189, led by the kings of England, France, and Germany. The German king accidentally drowned on the way, the other two kings quarreled, and that effort failed to retake the holy city.

In 1204, the army of the Fourth Crusade reached Constantinople, capital of the Byzantine Empire, on the way to the Holy Land. The Crusade's leaders fell into a fierce argument with Byzantine leaders, and as a result, the crusaders attacked the city. They captured it, looted many

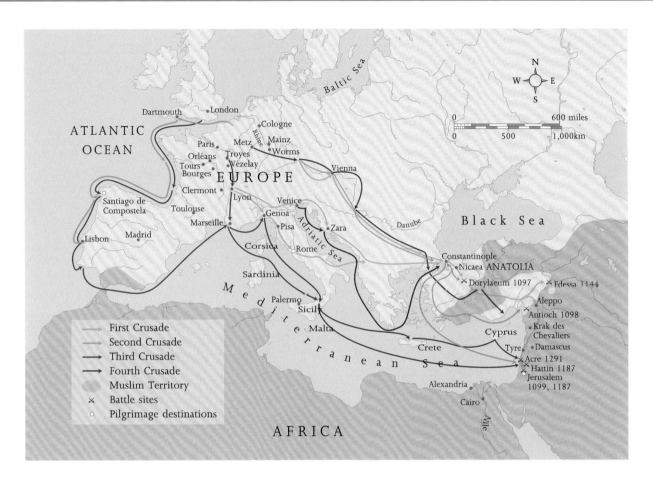

▲ In the First Crusade, crusader victories at Dorylaeum and Antioch, both in present-day Turkey, led to the capture of Jerusalem. Muslims retook Jerusalem in 1187 after defeating the crusaders at the Battle of Hattin. One hundred years later, they captured the last crusader stronghold, Acre, in 1291.

of its treasures, and removed the emperor from power. The Byzantines retook the city in 1261. In the thirteenth century, the crusading spirit dimmed. Three later crusades were also mounted, but they all failed. The Muslims overran the last Crusader stronghold in 1291.

Results of the Crusades

It is often said that the Crusades opened trade between Christian and Muslim lands. In truth, trade was already lively before the Crusades. Sometimes the Crusades are said to have brought Muslim learning into Christian lands. In fact, the conquests of Spain and Sicily played a far greater role in that. The movement certainly did not

the Children's Crusade

One of the strangest episodes of the Crusades was the so-called Children's Crusade. By the early thirteenth century, the crusading movement had lost its zeal. Some people thought that the Christian world should rely on the innocent and mild—children—to succeed where men at arms had failed. Thousands of young boys and girls marched from France and Germany to the Mediterranean. They expected God to part the waters of the sea so they could cross safely to Jerusalem. Many children died on the journey. Many more were captured and sold into slavery. The rest returned, disheartened.

unite Europe's rulers; they bickered and fought one another during and after the Crusades.

The Crusades did have two effects, however, and both were negative. The attack on Constantinople hurt the Byzantine Empire. Although the empire lasted two more centuries, it was smaller and weaker. Also, the wars in the Holy Land deepened the mistrust and bitter feelings between Christians and Muslims.

Building for God

Religious zeal led to the Crusades. It also led to the building of the magnificent cathedrals that stand as a symbol of medieval culture.

A cathedral is a bishop's church. For centuries, cathedrals had been built in a relatively simple style. After A.D. 1000, a new style appeared. It was called Romanesque because it used some of the building techniques that had been used in ancient Rome. The style produced large churches with massive walls and smallish windows. The buildings were larger and more impressive than those built in earlier centuries. Their somewhat dark interiors produced a feeling of religious mystery.

Builders wanted to bring more light into churches. The Gothic style, developed in the mid-twelfth century, achieved that goal. Builders used new techniques to build higher and higher ceilings—many more than 100 feet (about 30 meters). Because these ceilings were made of lighter materials, they could make lighter, thinner walls. They studded the soaring walls with dazzling glass windows. Some of these windows were round and decorated like blooming flowers. Others were made to show pictures that illustrated stories from the Bible or the lives of saints.

The Gothic style began around Paris in the mid-twelfth century and spread quickly. In France alone, dozens of cathedrals were built in the next decades. Huge amounts of stone were needed for this building campaign. From 1050 to about 1350, the French used more stone to build cathedrals than was used in the entire history

A Community Effort

Each cathedral took many years to build, and each expressed a town's pride. Many skilled craftspeople played a part. Working carefully, stone masons cut and fit the stones. Carpenters built scaffolds the masons had to stand on so they could stack the stones higher and higher into the air. Working away from the building site, glassmakers created the stained-glass windows. Sculptors decorated columns with statues of Jesus, the apostles, and other figures from the Bible. Many people contributed in different ways. Nobles gave money to fund windows that paid tribute to favorite saints. Cloth workers, tanners, and other workers also raised money to pay for windows, which sometimes showed them at their work.

of ancient Egypt. Other nations adopted the style as well, with local builders using special touches that showed local tastes.

Intellectual Growth

While cathedrals were being built, Church thinkers began exploring great questions of faith. Some of their thinking was just as dazzling as the new Gothic churches.

The Church had been committed to learning from the start. Church officials needed to write clearly to explain Church teachings. Monks in monasteries copied important writings about the religion to save them for later generations to read.

In the twelfth and thirteenth centuries, there was a new burst of intellectual activity. One reason was the new chance to read ancient Greek works that were now available in western Europe after the conquest of Muslim lands in Spain and southern Italy. Another cause was the rise of schools that were part of some of the great cathedrals. These schools eventually gave rise to the first universities. In these universities, scholars gathered to study law, medicine, and—most importantly—**theology**.

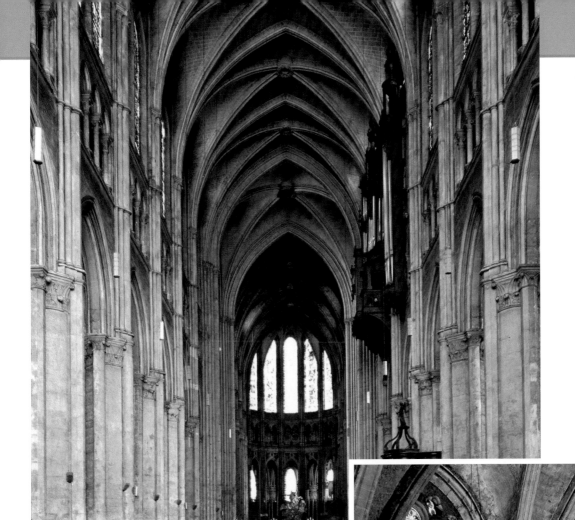

▲ The interior of Chartres Cathedral (*above*) shows the soaring ceilings and feeling of lightness that marked the Gothic style. The photograph on the right reveals some of the stained-glass windows that filled the high walls of Chartres and other Gothic cathedrals.

THE PURPOSE OF STAINED GLASS

"[We will fill the church] with the most radiant windows . . . [to] illumine people's minds so that they may travel through light to an apprehension of God's light."
Abbot Suger, *De Consecratione Ecclesiae*, 1140s [6]

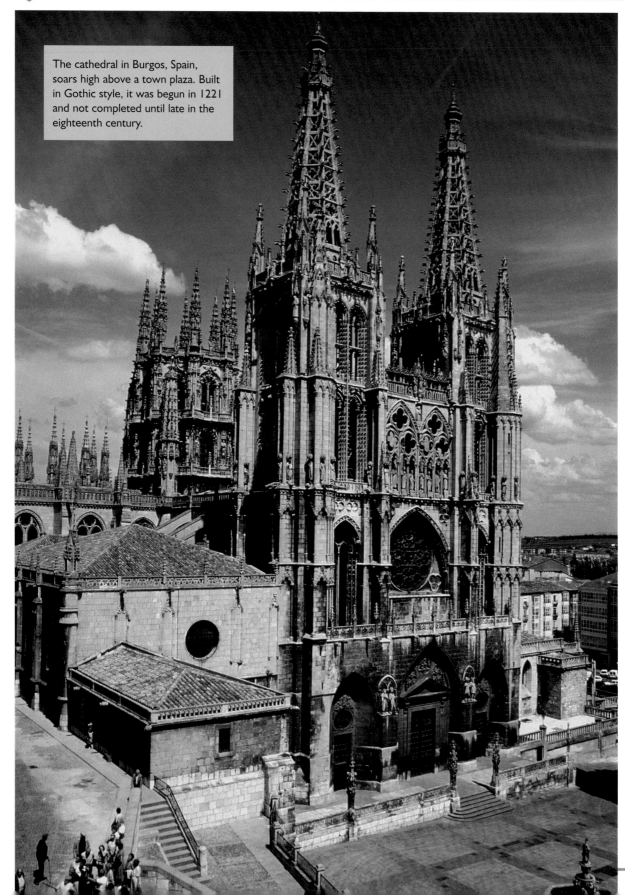

The cathedral in Burgos, Spain, soars high above a town plaza. Built in Gothic style, it was begun in 1221 and not completed until late in the eighteenth century.

◀ Thomas Aquinas, seated, instructs a group of students.

Those who studied theology developed a way of thinking called **scholasticism**. They tried to use logic to find a rational basis for faith. This drive was, in effect, another kind of crusade. The crusaders had used weapons to conquer Muslim lands. The scholastics wanted to use reason to show that Christianity was more logical than Islam.

The leading scholastic was Thomas Aquinas. The scholastics collected their writings into books of many volumes called summa. Aquinas's summa was on the subject of theology. He argued that the mind can apply reason to the knowledge gained from the senses and prove the existence of God.

thomas Aquinas
(c. 1224–1274)

Born in Italy, Thomas Aquinas became the foremost philosopher of the Middle Ages. Aquinas was placed by his family in a monastery while still young. After several years, he was sent to the University of Naples. There he read some of the works of ancient Greek philosophy that were just reaching Christian Europe from former Muslim lands. Excited by what he read, Aquinas continued his studies. By 1256, he began to teach at the University of Paris. For the rest of his life, he lived in the midst of a swirling current of ideas that tried to see how both faith and reason could lead to the truth. After his death, the Catholic Church ruled that some of his ideas were wrong. Later, though, his writings were adopted as Church **doctrine**, and he was made a saint.

CHAPTER 5

Challenges to the Church

any challenges to the Church plagued the Roman Catholic religion in the late Middle Ages. Some people called for a simpler way of life and openly criticized the Church. The writings of mystics who claimed that they had had religious experiences and direct contact with God seemed to make the Church unnecessary. Meanwhile, amid charges of corruption and unfair politics, the papacy fell into chaos.

Back to Basics

The growing power and wealth of the Roman Catholic Church seemed to go against the teachings of Jesus to some Christians. They rejected Church practices and authority in an effort to lead a more humble life that they thought showed greater devotion to God.

In the 1170s, Peter Waldo, a wealthy merchant in Lyons, France, heard the story of a saint who had adopted poverty. Inspired, he decided to

▼ This wall painting from a church in Florence shows Pope Innocent III giving his blessing to Francis of Assisi and his rule for Franciscan friars.

ORDERED POVERTY

"[The Poor Clares] are not to receive or hold onto any possessions or property . . . except as much land as necessity requires for the integrity and the proper seclusion of the monastery; and this land is not to be cultivated except as a garden for the needs of the sisters."
Clare of Assisi, *Rule*, 1212 [7]

follow the example. He began preaching in public to convince others to adopt this simpler life. Soon Waldo gathered a following, called Waldensians.

The same impulse moved Francis of Assisi, a deeply religious man, in the early thirteenth century. Francis, the son of an Italian merchant, began giving his money and clothing to the poor and sick. Eventually, he decided to found a new order within the Catholic Church. He called his followers *friars*, from the Latin for "brothers." Francis's rules for the order were strict. Brothers had to preach and work for the poor every day. They wore simple brown robes and owned as few possessions as possible. They could not even touch money and had to beg each day for shelter and food. Francis wanted them to carry the message of God to the people and inspire others to belief through their example of poverty.

The Franciscan order grew rapidly. Formed in 1210, more than fourteen hundred houses for the friars had been founded by 1300. Francis's example inspired a follower named Clare to found a similar order for women. The Poor Clares, as they were called, also spread quickly. There was a difference, though. Franciscans were active in the world, preaching in the cities. The Church did not want single women moving about in public, and they made the Poor Clares live in seclusion.

Some people adopted lives of poverty without withdrawing from the world. Women called Beguines dedicated themselves to helping the

▲ Clare of Assisi, shown here, was named a saint by the Church just two years after her death in 1253.

poor and sick. Some men joined this movement as well; they were called *Beghards*.

Fighting Heretics

The Church eyed some of these movements warily. Groups like the Franciscans who recognized obedience to the Church were welcome. The Waldensians, though, preached against Church officials for being more interested in wealth than matters of the spirit. Not surprisingly, their beliefs were labeled as heresy. The Church made some efforts to end the movement, but it survived by meeting in secret.

The Church also attacked other movements, especially the Cathars of southern France. This group believed that two gods, one good and one evil, struggled to rule the world. The Cathars said the Church followed the evil god. In 1209, Pope

the Inquisition

To root out heresy, the Catholic Church created what became a famous system of trials called the Inquisition. Over the years, the Inquisition gained a frightening reputation. Trials were held in secret. Witnesses who spoke against accused **heretics** did so without the accused person's knowledge. Since defending a heretic was itself a crime, no lawyers were willing to help the accused. Torture was permitted as a way of winning a confession. The penalty for guilt was death. In the Middle Ages, however, Inquisition trials led to the execution of only about two thousand people. More were victims in later periods. An order of friars—the Dominicans—often carried out the trials. Founded by a Castilian, Domingo de Guzman, this order devoted itself to learning theology. Church leaders believed that the Dominicans' deep study put them in a position to identify heresy. Their skill at exposing heretics produced a popular pun on their names. The Dominicans were sometimes called by the Latin words *Domini canes*, which means "hounds of the lord (or God)."

Innocent III called for a crusade against them and used Church funds to finance the army. Soldiers marched into southern France and killed tens of thousands of Cathars.

In the mid-fourteenth century, John Wycliffe of England preached that the Church should return to its roots and adopt poverty. He, too, rejected the authority of Church officials. Thinking that all believers should have access to the Word of God, he urged that the Bible be translated from Latin into common languages, such as English. After his death, Wycliffe's ideas were condemned as heresy. Church officials sought out and punished his followers.

Wycliffe's ideas, however, had reached Bohemia in central Europe. In about 1400, they were adopted by a preacher named John Hus. The Hussite movement grew popular and was seen as increasingly dangerous. Some of Hus's followers wanted to weaken the hold of the Holy Roman Empire on their land. This threat to both the Church and the rule of Emperor Sigismund was too great to be allowed to continue. The Church called Hus to a Church council. There he was seized, convicted of heresy, and burned at the stake. Hus's execution ignited a revolt in Bohemia.

Church Mystics

Some pious Christians—called mystics—had deep and life-changing religious experiences. Through these experiences, they felt that they achieved union with God. This message of direct contact with God sometimes alarmed Church officials. Meister Eckhart was a popular German preacher. Although he was a Dominican, the Church condemned some of his ideas as heretical. Marguerite Porete of France—another mystic—was tried in Paris and executed by the Inquisition.

◀ This illustration shows French soldiers driving defeated Cathars out of the city of Carcassonne, in southern France. This city was one of the strongholds of the Cathar movement.

A MYSTIC'S NEAR-DEATH EXPERIENCE

"When I was thirty years old and a half, God sent me a bodily sickness, in which I lay three days and three nights; and on the fourth night I took all my rites of Holy Church, and [expected] not to have lived till day.

I . . . set my eyes on the face of the Crucifix. . . . After this my sight began to fail, and it was all dark about me in the chamber, as if it had been night, save in the image of the Cross whereon I beheld a common light. . . . And in this [moment] suddenly all my pain was taken from me, and I was as whole . . . as ever I was before."
Julian of Norwich, *Revelations of Divine Love,* **c. 1400** [8]

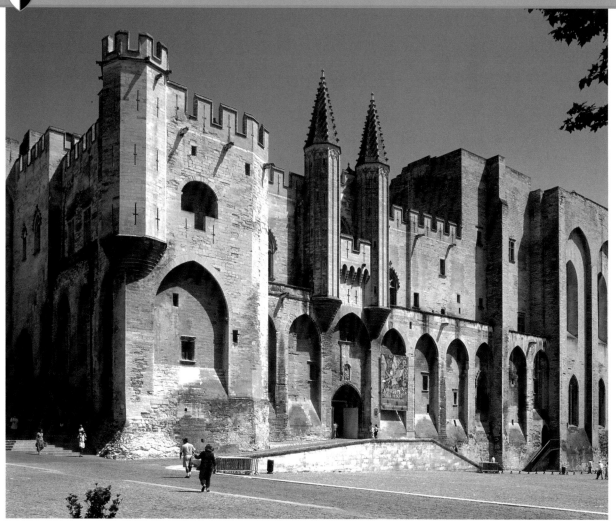

▲ The palace used by the popes at Avignon, shown here, looks more like a fortress than a palace.

Many mystics were left alone, however, and some even enjoyed honored status within the Church. A woman named Julian of Norwich lived as an anchoress at the cathedral at Norwich, England, until her seventies. Hildegard of Bingen, a German nun and a mystic, was highly respected. Heads of monasteries asked her advice. Members of the clergy also sought her views on theology.

Discredit and Schism

While the Roman Catholic Church was challenged by heretics, serious problems beset the papacy. In 1309, Pope Clement V moved himself and the government of the Church to Avignon, a city in France. For nearly seventy years, he and several succeeding popes led the Catholic Church from this city, not Rome. The popes lost some moral authority in these years. One reason was that they tended to favor France in disputes between countries. As a result, they could no longer claim that they treated everyone equally. Another factor was the rich and luxurious life led by Church officials in France.

What followed was even worse. In 1378, Pope Gregory XI returned to Rome but died soon after. After Urban VI was elected, the cardinals turned against him. They moved back to Avignon, declared his election null, and chose a new pope, Clement VII. From 1378 to 1415, two rival popes headed the Roman Catholic Church, one from Rome and one from Avignon. Political rivalries in Europe shaped which pope different rulers chose to follow. France and its allies favored Clement. England, Germany, and other countries sided with Urban. For the next several decades, the Church was split by the conflicting orders of rival popes. This division is called the Great Schism (a *schism* is a break). Starting in 1409 there was even a third pope, based in Pisa, Italy. He was Alexander V, and he had been elected by a Church council.

Restoring Order in the Church

The problem of multiple popes was finally settled in 1415. The Holy Roman Emperor Sigismund and Pope John XXII—who had succeeded

Alexander V in Pisa—called a Church council. Bishops from across Europe met in Constance, Germany. John XXII took part at first but then fled the city, hoping his departure would leave the council without authority—and leave him in power. Emperor Sigismund forced the council to continue working without John XXII. In the end, it agreed to unseat all three popes and elect a new one.

The new pope, Martin V, brought the papacy back to Rome. During his rule, he summoned other councils. They made decisions that Church leaders in all lands agreed to follow. This helped reunite the Church. The papacy had become weakened by all the disputes, however. Councils became very important in leading the Church in the next few decades.

◄ Emperor Sigismund, shown here, was vital to the success of the Council of Constance. He wanted it to not only solve the problem of the popes but move against John Hus. Hus's followers were causing turmoil in Bohemia, part of Sigismund's empire. Sigismund wanted the Church to condemn the Hussites so he could have the backing of its authority to crack down on them.

CHAPTER 6

Other faiths

atholic Christianity was not the only faith of medieval Europe. In the Byzantine Empire and other lands in eastern Europe, people followed the Eastern Orthodox Church. Muslims ruled some lands on the northern shores of the Mediterranean. Jews lived scattered throughout Europe, where they sometimes faced harsh treatment from Christians.

Differing Churches

During the early days of Christianity, churches in the eastern and western halves of the Roman Empire differed in many ways. Some differences were central to their beliefs. They disagreed on the exact relationship of the three aspects of God—the Father, the Son, and the Holy Spirit. They argued about what kind of bread should be used in the Mass. Even the date for celebrating Easter was a matter of dispute. They also differed over leadership. Bishops in western churches were guided by the pope, the bishop of Rome. Those in the east paid more attention to the patriarch, the title given the bishop of Constantinople.

The split between the two groups of churches became final in 1054. That year, Pope Leo IX and Patriarch Michael Cerularius had angrily excommunicated each other. The Church in the west came to be called the Roman Catholic Church. The eastern Church became the Eastern Orthodox Church.

The Eastern Orthodox Church was closely linked to the Byzantine Empire. Emperors had some influence on the Church and on the naming of Church officials. Emperors, however, were not allowed to make decisions about major beliefs in the Church.

As in the west, the Eastern Orthodox Church tried to convert people who were pagans. Missionaries went to present-day Russia, Ukraine, Bulgaria, and other regions to convert people. As churches developed in these areas, each had its own chief bishop, who went to Church councils. In the Eastern Orthodox Church, these councils had the highest authority. The patriarch commanded the respect of the other bishops, but they did not have to obey him. The patriarch, then, had less power over the Eastern Orthodox Church than the pope had over the Roman Catholic Church.

A focal point of the Eastern Orthodox Church was the impressive cathedral called the Hagia

▲ This fourteenth-century Russian painting of Saint Demetrius shows the influence in Russia of the art of the Byzantine Empire. When the Russians converted to the Eastern Orthodox faith, they adopted Byzantine culture.

▲ The Hagia Sophia (*above*) still stands in Istanbul, formerly known as Constantinople, in Turkey. Today it serves as a mosque, but some decorations, such as a mosaic portrait of Jesus, show its origins as a Christian church.

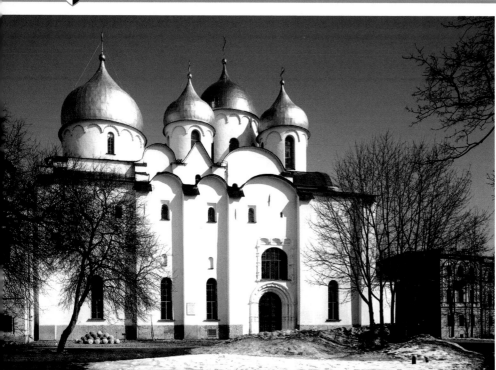

◀ Onion-shaped domes top the towers of many Russian churches, such as this cathedral in the city of Novgorod.

Converting the Slavs

In the ninth century, the monks Cyril and Methodius were dispatched from Constantinople to present-day Bulgaria and nearby lands, where they converted the Slavs. In the process, they invented an alphabet for writing Slavic so they could translate the Gospels into that language. That system—called Cyrillic after one of the monks—is still used in Russia and other Slavic lands today. Russia joined the Eastern Orthodox Church in the tenth century, when Prince Vladimir of Kiev adopted the faith.

Sophia, or the Church of the Holy Wisdom. It was built in Constantinople by Justinian, emperor of the Byzantine Empire in the mid-sixth century. For many centuries, it was the most magnificent church in the entire Christian world.

A New Religion: Islam

Starting in the eighth century, the Byzantine Empire was seriously challenged by a series of conquests made in the name of a new religion, Islam. Followers of Islam believed that the founder of the religion, Muhammad, received revelations from God. Born in about 570, Muhammad proclaimed that there was only one God, Allah, and that people had to submit to God's will. *Muslim*, the term for believers in Islam, means "one who submits."

In the early seventh century, Muhammad's faith spread quickly across the Arabian peninsula. Within a century, Muslim armies had conquered a huge stretch of land from modern Iran to Spain and all along the eastern and southern shores of the Mediterranean. Eventually they also took parts of southern Italy.

Muslim law united the different peoples living in this huge territory. The Arabic language linked them as well. Arabic was the language of the Koran—the Muslim holy book. Muslims believed that the words of Allah could only be understood by reading them in Arabic. Converts learned Arabic, then, to better understand the faith and to take part in prayers.

Muslims—like Christians—believed that their

religion was the one, true faith and that only believers would enjoy eternal happiness in paradise. Still, they did not try to win converts in the same way Christians did. Those people who wished to convert could convert; it was a matter of choice. Non-Muslims quickly noticed, however, that Muslims had more privileges than they. That fact led many non-Muslims to adopt the faith.

In Islam, Christians have special status because Muhammad recognized Jesus as a worthy prophet. In Muslim-held lands in the

The Five Pillars of Islam

Five practices show a Muslim's devotion to Islam. They are:

  Making a declaration of faith: "There is no God but Allah, and Muhammad is his messenger."

  Praying five times a day, every day

  Donating money to charity, which is used to care for the poor

  Fasting during daylight hours each day of the holy month of Ramadan

  Making a pilgrimage to the holy city of Mecca, in today's Saudi Arabia, at least once, if possible

Middle Ages, Christians had to pay the same tax all non-Muslims had to pay, but they enjoyed some privileges other non-Muslims did not. They were usually allowed to worship as they wished, though they could not try to convert Muslims. Christians were usually not persecuted, either. Many Christians in Muslim lands decided to convert to Islam. In fact, the majority of the population in Spain became Muslim.

Christian treatment of Muslims followed similar patterns. In some periods, they were tolerated and allowed to practice their religion. For instance, as Christian rulers in Spain and southern Italy took Muslim lands, they often left Muslims alone. Over time, though, Muslims living in Spain and southern Italy suffered harsher treatment. Some converted to Christianity, sometimes because they were forced to do so by rulers, and others left for Muslim lands.

Jews in Muslim and Christian Lands

The Muslims who ruled Spain and southern Italy generally tolerated Jews in their lands as well. Islam sees the prophets of the Old Testament, on which the Jewish religion is largely based, as part of its tradition. Muslim Spain had a thriving

◀ This miniature painting from the late fifteenth century shows Muslims at school. The walls, as in many rooms in Muslim buildings, are decorated with complex patterns.

▲ These columns form part of the interior of the magnificent mosque built by Muslim rulers in Córdoba, Spain, from 785 to 990. After Christians took the city in the thirteenth century, they turned the building into a cathedral.

Moses Maimonides
(1135-1204)

The Jewish philosopher Moses Maimonides was born in Muslim Spain. When he was in his teens, the Almohads took power, and his family eventually left. He spent the rest of his life in North Africa and Europe. Trained as a physician, he was also a rabbi, or Jewish religious teacher. In that role, he wrote an important book about Jewish law. Maimonides is most famous, though, for his book *A Guide for the Perplexed*, which he finished in 1191. In it, he tried to reconcile reason and religion. The book was widely read by both Jewish and Christian thinkers.

Jewish community, which enjoyed something of a golden age in the tenth to the early twelfth centuries. Leading Jews served as close advisors to Muslim rulers. Many Jews thrived in the booming economy. Physicians advanced their science, and philosophers thought and wrote about the nature of faith. Jewish poets wrote moving poems that helped keep the Hebrew language alive.

That golden age ended in the early twelfth century, when a more extreme group of Muslims called the Almohads came to power in Spain. The Almohads forced Jews to convert to Islam or leave the country. Some Jews pretended to convert but continued to practice Judaism secretly. Many left, traveling to other Muslim lands or to Christian kingdoms in Spain or elsewhere in Europe.

In most of Christian Europe, Jews lived difficult lives. They were not always persecuted; sometimes they were grudgingly tolerated, but they always lived on the edge of society, unable to predict when rulers or common people would turn against them.

Sometimes they were subjected to vicious attacks. The first major one came in 1095 during the First Crusade. On their way to the Holy Land, an army of crusading knights attacked Jews in several German towns. They massacred many people, including men, women, and children. They also robbed, taking all the victims' valuables. This was not the last time that Jews suffered such attacks. The worst violence came in the middle to late fourteenth century, when the **Black Death** raged across Europe. In some areas, Jews were falsely accused of causing the deadly disease by poisoning wells. Mobs in many towns from Germany to Spain killed innocent Jews.

Even where they were allowed to live, Jews were often treated unfairly. Laws blocked them from entering some professions. Other laws forced them to live only in certain areas in towns. The Catholic Church ruled in 1215 that all Jews had to wear special badges on their clothing to identify them. Sometimes rulers forced them to leave the country, which happened in England in 1290 and in France in 1306. In both cases, the reason was simply royal greed—the kings seized their lands and property to enrich themselves.

For many centuries, the lives of Jews in Spain were somewhat better. When Christian kings took land from Muslim rulers, they continued to allow Jews to practice their religion. One Christian king, Peter IV, let the Jews of Toledo build a new **synagogue**. Later, though, the position of Jews became more difficult. In a sudden eruption of violence, thousands of Jews were killed in 1391. The cause was another outbreak of the Black Death, for which Jews were once again wrongly

▲ In this illustration from a 1350 manuscript from Barcelona, Spain, a Jewish family celebrates the religious holiday of Passover. During Passover, Jews recall the time thousands of years ago when God freed them from slavery in Egypt. During the Middle Ages, Jews did not live in slavery, as they had in ancient Egypt, but they were often persecuted and sometimes expelled from the lands where they lived.

blamed. In later years, many Spanish Jews were forced to convert to Christianity. Even then, the converts were not trusted as being true Christians. Finally, in 1492, all Jews were expelled from Spain.

Spain also forced Muslims to leave the country or to convert to Christianity. The change seemed to be a great triumph for the Spanish rulers—and for the Roman Catholic Church. In the next century, though, the Catholic hold on Europe would be broken by the Protestant Reformation. That movement saw millions of people move into new churches that were being formed. Nevertheless, in this later period, as during the Middle Ages, religion remained a vital part of European life.

312
Constantine declares Christianity legal in the Roman Empire.

325
Constantine calls Church council at Nicaea.

380
Theodosius I makes Christianity the official religion in the Roman Empire.

476
The end of the reign of the last Roman emperor in western Europe marks the end of the Roman Empire.

537
Hagia Sophia, a Christian church, is completed in Constantinople, now known as Istanbul.

622
Muhammad moves to the city of Medina and recruits followers, marking the beginning of Islam.

711
Muslims enter Iberia and begin the conquest of Spain.

c. 755
The Papal States are created. This is the territory in Italy controlled by the pope.

900s
Fears rise that the Day of Judgment is coming when the millenium ends.

900s-1100s
The Jews in Muslim Spain prosper during a "Golden Age."

965
Muslim forces capture Sicily and some of southern Italy.

1000s
Religious feeling becomes more intense through much of Europe and the number of people going on pilgrimages increases.

1049
Pope Leo IX becomes the first of several reformer popes.

1054
The Roman Catholic Church and Eastern Orthodox Church split.

1070s
Pope Gregory VII and King Henry IV of Germany clash over investiture issue.

1075-1125
The period when churches are built in the Romanesque style in western Europe.

1091
The Normans complete the takeover of Muslim Sicily.

1095
Pope Urban II calls for a crusade; the First Crusade begins the following year.

1099
Crusaders capture Jerusalem, and the success of the First Crusade leads to the creation of the Crusader States in the Holy Land.

1137-1144
The church of Saint-Denis, near Paris, France—the first Gothic church in Europe—is constructed.

1122
An agreement between Pope Callistus II and Emperor Henry V ends the investiture conflict.

1204
Crusaders of the Fourth Crusade take Constantinople.

1209-1229
The Church carries out a crusade against the Cathars in southern France.

1209
Pope Innocent III approves the Franciscan order.

1212
Thousands of French and German children go on the Children's Crusade, which collapses.

1216
Pope Honorius III approves the Dominican order, whose members lived in poverty.

1256
Thomas Aquinas begins teaching at the University of Paris.

1291
Muslims capture Acre, the last Crusader city.

1309
Clement V moves papacy to Avignon, France.

1347
The plague, or Black Death, breaks out for the first time in medieval Europe.

1378-1415
The period known as the Great Schism, during which time rival popes rule in both Rome and Avignon.

1391
Anti-Jewish violence in Spain results in the death of thousands of Jews.

1411
John Wycliffe's works are declared full of heresy.

1414-1418
Council of Constance meets, reforming the Church. The Council also declares John Hus a heretic and executes him.

1453
Muslim Ottoman Turks capture Constantinople, ending the Byzantine Empire.

1492
Isabella and Ferdinand capture Granada, the last Muslim possession in Spain, marking the end of the Reconquista.

Source References:

[1] **C. Warren Hollister,** *Medieval Europe: A Short History*, **Wiley, 1964, p. 1.**

[2] **Alcuin of York. Quoted in J. A. Hoeppner Moran Cruz and R. Gerberding,** *see above,* **p. 193.**

[3] **Council of Narbonne. Quoted in J. A. Hoeppner Moran Cruz and R. Gerberding,** *see above,* **p. 267.**

[4] **Gelasius I. Quoted in J. A. Hoeppner Moran Cruz and R. Gerberding,** *see above,* **p. 278.**

[5] **Gesta Francorum. Quoted in J. A. Hoeppner Moran Cruz and R. Gerberding,** *see above,* **p. 299.**

[6] **Abbot Suger. Quoted in the web site of the Archdiocese of Detroit, Cathedral of the Most Blessed Sacrament section, "A Cathedral Narrative."**

[7] **Clare of Assisi Rule. Quoted in J. A. Hoeppner Moran Cruz and R. Gerberding,** *see above,* **p. 434.**

[8] **Julian of Norwich. Quoted from Chapter III of** *The Revelations of Divine Love* **in the Christian Classics Ethereal Library at the Calvin College web site.**

[9] **Quoted in E. Peters,** *Europe and the Middle Ages,* **second edition, Prentice Hall, 1989, p. 65.**

anchorites/anchoresses People who decide to live a secluded life away from others in a small cell and devote themselves to prayer

apostles The twelve closest followers of Jesus, who traveled with him as he preached and who spread belief in him after his death

baptized Blessed a person with water in a Christian rite that symbolizes the person's acceptance into the Christian Church

barbarian An ancient Greek word used by Romans and later Europeans to describe foreigners. It suggests that foreigners are wild, brutal, and savage.

Black Death Name given to the bubonic plague, a disease that swept across Europe in the mid-fourteenth century and returned several times thereafter. It killed huge numbers of people, perhaps as much as one-third to one-half of Europe's population.

Byzantine Empire The empire that had been the eastern part of the Roman Empire and was based in Constantinople and lasted until 1453.

caravans Travelers who group together to help each other, usually in a hostile region, such as a desert

clergy People recognized by the Church as having the authority to perform religious services

convert A person who has adopted a new religion

Crusades Wars fought between Christians and Muslims, pagans, or heretics

doctrine An official system of religious belief

excommunicated Declared that a member of the Church has done something so wrong that he or she is officially expelled from it; loyal Church members were supposed to avoid contact with that person and no longer owed him or her obedience.

Germanic Related to German-speaking peoples, such as the Goths, Visigoths, and Franks, who moved into western Europe in the later centuries of the Roman Empire and set up several new kingdoms after the fall of the western Roman Empire

Gothic A style of church architecture developed in the mid-twelfth century marked by very tall churches, relatively thin stone walls, narrow column supports, pointed arches, and large amounts of stained glass

heresy A belief that differs from official Church beliefs

heretics People who disagree with or dissent from established religious beliefs

Holy Land The areas of modern Israel and the West Bank believed to be holy by Christians because Jesus Christ lived and taught there

Iberian Refers to the region of southwestern Europe that is now occupied by Spain and Portugal

lay investiture Right of a ruler to appoint people to high Church positions without the approval of the pope

martyred Put to death for one's beliefs or faith

Mass The rite that includes the ritual eating of bread and drinking of wine that is part of Roman Catholic services; the two substances symbolize the body and blood of Jesus, and the ritual recalls the last meal he shared with his apostles.

medieval A word that relates to and describes the Middle Ages

monasteries Communities of clergymen, called monks, who pray, work, and live according to a strict rule

Norman A member of a Viking tribe who settled in northern France

pagans A term used by Christians to refer to the religions of the Romans and Germanic peoples, who worshiped many gods; now means person with no religion

papacy The office of the pope and all the parts of the administration of the Roman Catholic Church that the pope controls

parishioners People who live in a parish (the area attached to a church)

parliament A conference to discuss public affairs, or the organization of political groups to form a government

penance Actions that a person can take to win forgiveness of his or her sins

persecuted Caused to suffer because of one's beliefs

pilgrimages Journeys by individuals or groups to a place of religious importance

relics Physical remains of a holy person's life, which might include the bones or blood of a saint or objects that the saint used or touched. In the Middle Ages, people believed relics could work miracles.

Roman Empire The people and lands that belonged to ancient Rome, consisting of most of southern Europe and northern Africa from Britain to the Middle East

saints People identified by the Church as especially holy; ordinary people pray to them, asking for help with particular problems or concerns

scholasticism School of philosophy of the late Middle Ages that tried to use logic to find a rational basis for faith

simony Buying or selling of a position within a church

synagogue Jewish house of worship

theology The study of religious faiths

further Information

Books:

Atkinson, Kenneth. *Judaism* (Religions of the World). Philadelphia: Chelsea House, 2004.

Cartlidge, Cherese. *The Crusades: Failed Holy Wars* (History's Great Defeats). San Diego: Lucent Books, 2002.

Clark, Charles. *Islam* (Religions of the World). San Diego: Greenhaven Press, 2001.

Hallick, Mary P. *The Story of Icons.* Holy Cross Press, 2001.

Hinds, Kathryn. *The Church* (Life in the Middle Ages). New York: Benchmark Books, 2000.

Lace, William W. *The Medieval Cathedral* (Building History Series). San Diego: Lucent, 2001.

Web Sites:

The Middle Ages
www.learner.org/exhibits/middleages
This web site is created for the Annenberg Foundation and the Corporation for Public Broadcasting. It has information on various medieval topics, including religion.

NetSERF (The Internet Connection for Medieval Resources)
www.netserf.org
This web site has many links organized by topic. Check the topics under the headings "Philosophy" and "Religion" and also "Cathedrals and Churches" (under "Architecture") and "Saints and Martyrs" (under "Women").

Videos/DVDs:

Chartres Cathedral: A Sacred Geometry. Janson Video, 2002 (DVD).

Christianity: The First Thousand Years and Christianity: The Second Thousand Years. A&E Entertainment, 2001 (VHS, DVD).

Islam: Empire of Faith. PBS Home Video, 2001 (VHS, DVD).

The Middle Ages. Goldhil Video, 2001 (VHS).

The Popes: The Legacy of Peter. A&E Entertainment, 2005 (VHS, DVD).

Your Oral or Multimedia Presentation

by Lisa Bullard

Enslow Elementary

an imprint of

Enslow Publishers, Inc.

40 Industrial Road
Box 398
Berkeley Heights, NJ 07922
USA

http://www.enslow.com

For my elementary school teacher Beverly Henriques, who so encouraged me.

Enslow Elementary, an imprint of Enslow Publishers, Inc.

Enslow Elementary® is a registered trademark of Enslow Publishers, Inc.

Copyright © 2009 by Enslow Publishers, Inc.

Library of Congress Cataloging-in-Publication Data
Bullard, Lisa.
   Ace your oral or multimedia presentation / Lisa Bullard.
      p. cm. — (Ace it! information literacy series)
   Includes bibliographical references and index.
   Summary: "Learn how to research, write, practice, and present an oral or multimedia presentation with confidence"—Provided by publisher.
   ISBN-13: 978-0-7660-3391-7
   ISBN-10: 0-7660-3391-0
   1. Public speaking—Juvenile literature. 2. Multimedia systems—Juvenile literature. I. Title.
   PN4129.15.B85 2009
   808.5'1—dc22
                                    2008024885

Printed in the United States of America

10 9 8 7 6 5 4 3 2 1

To Our Readers:
We have done our best to make sure all Internet Addresses in this book were active and appropriate when we went to press. However, the author and the publisher have no control over and assume no liability for the material available on those Internet sites or on other Web sites they may link to. Any comments or suggestions can be sent by e-mail to comments@enslow.com or to the address on the back cover.

♻ Enslow Publishers, Inc., is committed to printing our books on recycled paper. The paper in every book contains 10% to 30% post-consumer waste (PCW). The cover board on the outside of each book contains 100% PCW. Our goal is to do our part to help young people and the environment too!

Cover photo: PhotoEdit/David Young-Wolff; iStockphoto.com/Jim Pruitt (background).
Interior photos: Alamy/Bill Watson, p. 32; Associated Press Images, p. 10; Corbis/Tim Pannell, p. 12; Getty Images/Dirk Anschutz, p. 38; The Image Works/Jim West, p. 20; iStockphoto.com/Andres Peiro, pp. 3, 5, 8, 13, 21, 27, 33, 35, 39; iStockphoto.com/Aldo Murillo, p. 9; iStockphoto.com/Christine Balderas, pp. 19, 25; iStockphoto.com/Mustafa Deliormanli, p. 22; iStockphoto.com/nsjulio, pp. 30 top right and bottom left, 31 center and center right; iStockphoto.com/Carmen Martínez, pp. 30 top left, 31 center left; iStockphoto.com/simon2579, pp. 30 bottom right, 31 bottom right; iStockphoto.com/René Mansi, p. 31 top right; iStockphoto.com/Eva Serrabassa, p. 31 top left; Jupiter Images/Corbis Premium, p. 29; Jupiter Images/Nonstock, p. 36; Photo Edit/Michael Newman, pp. 4, 26, 37; Photolibrary.com, pp. 16, 41; Rob Court, p. 28 illustration.

Contents

So You Have to Give a Presentation?

You just found out that you have to give a presentation. Is it for your teacher or for the school science fair? Or is it your turn to present something to your scout troop? Maybe you are competing in a poetry slam, or you're running for club president. How do you feel about speaking in front of an audience? Some people love to be the center of attention. If you like being in the spotlight, this book will show you how to be a power presenter.

For other people, giving a presentation is a little bit scary. Even many adults are nervous at the thought. If you are one of these people, don't worry. This book will give you tips to be a comfortable and confident presenter.

You may not know it, but you've probably already given a presentation. Have you ever brought something to school for show-and-tell? Have you given your swim team a pep talk? Those were presentations. A presentation happens anytime someone talks about information or ideas in front of an audience.

People use the skill of making presentations in many different ways. Educator Wendy Rubinyi says that summer camps often make multimedia presentations to show their programs to kids.[1] Maybe you have seen one of these. Perhaps you have seen a speech given by the president of the United States, or you've watched somebody famous give a presentation at your school. If you've heard a religious leader speak at a church or synagogue, that's a presentation, too.

People have different goals when they make presentations. Sometimes the goal is to teach something. You might give a report to tell your audience about a country or a famous person. You might teach the audience how to juggle or how to make a paper crane.

In other presentations, your goal is to communicate your ideas or feelings. You might tell the audience about something special that happened to you. Maybe you will describe your favorite book.

Sometimes presentations are persuasive. The presenter tries to convince the audience to have a certain opinion. For example, you might argue that cats make better pets than dogs. Perhaps you want to persuade your friends and relatives to donate money for your school fundraiser.

Other presentations are meant to be entertaining. They include acting out a play or doing a dramatic reading of a story or a poem. Your goal is to bring literature to life for the audience.

All presentations have one thing in common. They all give you a chance to connect with your audience and show your excitement about your topic. If you are bored with your presentation topic, your audience will also be bored. If you are enthusiastic about your topic, you can watch their eyes light up or hear their laughter. Your audience might even applaud because you have done such a good job!

Here are the steps for making a great presentation:

Steps for Making a Presentation

Step 1: Choose Your Topic

Step 2: Explore Your Topic

Step 3: Draft and Revise

Step 4: Add Visual Aids

Step 5: Rehearse and Present

Step 6: Review and Publish

Choose Your Topic

You're not quite ready for applause yet. You've got to start at **Step 1: Choose your topic**. What will you talk about in your presentation? Sometimes your topic will be assigned. For example, your teacher might ask you to read a certain poem or to talk about a specific book. Keep an open mind. Look for a way to make your topic fun.

Maybe you don't have an assignment at all! You get to choose what you'll talk about. In that case, start with something that interests you, and something that is a little bit familiar.

Step 1: Choose Your Topic

Step 2: Explore Your Topic

Step 3: Draft and Revise

Step 4: Add Visual Aids

Step 5: Rehearse and Present

Step 6: Review and Publish

What pops into your mind when you think about this topic? Make lists of ideas until you find an exciting topic for your presentation. This part is called brainstorming. Graphic organizers like the one on page 11 can be really helpful brainstorming tools. (In general, a graphic organizer is a chart or diagram that helps you plan ideas.)

Make sure not to forget about your audience. You want them to be interested in your topic, too. Will you be speaking in front of kids your age? They will

Picking the right topic can be a challenge. Find something you're excited to talk about.

probably enjoy many of the same things you do. Parents and grandparents usually appreciate presenters who are organized and well prepared. On the other hand, your audience might include judges you have never met before. Then you need to find out how they are going to judge you.

Think about how much your audience already knows about your topic. Will you need to give them basic information, or do they already understand a lot about your topic?

Think about all the parts of your assignment. Has your teacher given you a rubric? This is a guide that tells you how your presentation will be graded. How long is your presentation supposed to be? Will you get to use technology like a computer or a CD player? Can you wear a costume or bring in props? Answer these questions, and you are on your way to speaking success!

Could You Change History?

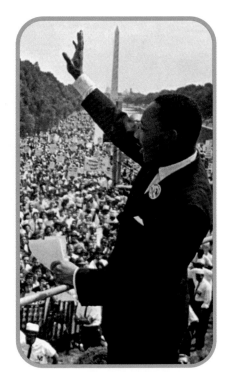

Presentations can change the world. Writer Alex Barnett says, "At every pivotal moment in American history you will find a great speech."[2] Have you ever heard the phrase "I have a dream"? Dr. Martin Luther King, Jr., used this phrase in one of his famous speeches. His powerful words changed people's minds and hearts. His speech changed the world.

Brainstorming for a Topic: Word Web

This is an example of a word web graphic organizer. In a word web, you start with your topic in the center. Then you think of words related to your topic. You keep branching out as you brainstorm for ideas.

Imagine that you're creating a presentation about a family vacation. Start by trying to remember every last detail.

Explore Your Topic

Now that you have chosen your topic, it is time for **Step 2: Explore your topic**. This is an important part of prewriting. Prewriting means getting prepared to write.

How will you explore your topic? It depends on what kind of presentation you're doing. If you will be talking about something familiar—like your family's vacation to Yellowstone Park—search your memory for every last detail. Close your eyes and imagine that you're back at Yellowstone. If you are doing a book report, you need to read the book carefully.

Step 1: Choose Your Topic

Step 2: Explore Your Topic

Step 3: Draft and Revise

Step 4: Add Visual Aids

Step 5: Rehearse and Present

Step 6: Review and Publish

13

If you are teaching your audience how to make something, you must figure out every step.

As you explore your topic, remember that you will be talking to an audience. You can begin to plan for this as well. If you are talking about your family's trip to Yellowstone Park, look for postcards or photographs to show your audience. Think ahead about your presentation as you explore.

Let's say you are doing a dramatic reading of a poem. There are many ways to explore this topic. If the poem has words you don't know, look them up in a dictionary. Then learn something about the author's life. For example, what did people wear when the author was alive? Maybe you could wear a costume to make your reading more powerful. Performance poet Sara Holbrook tells presenters to compare the poem to a memory from their own lives. Then, she says, "Let that memory become part of your performance."[3]

Many presentations require research. Research is the process of finding information about your topic. At this stage of prewriting, a graphic organizer can be very helpful. Try a KWHL chart like the one on the next page. You can use this to figure out what you need to learn about your topic. Fill in the last column as you do your research.

The library, also called a media center, is your research headquarters. It contains reference materials such as encyclopedias and atlases. There are books and magazines and newspapers. Trained media specialists (librarians) can help you find the facts you need.

[You can copy this chart onto another piece of paper to create your own. Do not write in this book!]

KWHL Chart

Fill in a chart like this to plan your research.

What I Already Know	What I Want to Find Out	How I Can Find It	What I Have Learned
—bald eagles have white heads —found in North America	—still endangered? —what do they eat?	—Web site —bird book	

The media specialist can also help you with computer research. This kind of research can be exciting. You will find articles to read and videos to see. You'll also find things to listen to. For instance, if your report is about bald eagles, you might find a recording of a bald eagle's call. Then you could add it to your presentation. There is also a whole world of information on the Internet. Ask an adult to explain your school or library's rules for going online.

Sometimes you will use the Internet to look up a specific Web site. Other times you will have to sort through millions of sites. Internet search engines, like Google, are good sorting tools. To do a search, enter your topic in the search bar. You can enter keywords—one or more words related to your topic. Once you hit the ENTER key, a list of Web sites will pop up. Click on the links to visit the different sites.

Are you finding the information you need? Look at your KWHL chart for other things to search. If you get only a few Web sites on your list, you will need to try more general keywords. For example, use *cookie recipes*

Media specialists are happy to help you with computer research.

instead of *oatmeal raisin chocolate chip cookie*. If you get too many sites on your list, you may have to add more specific keywords to narrow your search. For example, use *bald eagle* instead of *North American birds*.

Beware: you can't believe everything you read. This is especially true on the Internet! Look for Web sites from places like museums, zoos, universities, and government offices. These sites are more likely to have accurate, up-to-date information.

The best researchers use more than just the Internet. Find multiple types of sources when you can. Sometimes the sources will not agree. How do you know who is right? Check to see if most sources agree on one

Stay Safe Online

Exploring the Internet is like exploring a new universe. There are lots of exciting things to discover. There are also dangers, however. Some Web sites have information that is not appropriate for children. Get an adult's permission before you go online. Never post your last name, address, photograph, e-mail address, or phone number on a computer unless your parent or teacher tells you it is okay. If anyone asks you personal questions online, or if something makes you uncomfortable, leave the Web site and tell an adult right away.

answer. For some presentations, you might not find only one correct answer to a question. Instead, you will have to talk about many possible answers.

Remember that people can be sources, too. Perhaps your neighbor is a firefighter, and she can tell you about fire safety. Perhaps a local zookeeper can answer your questions about taking care of animals.

Set up an interview if your source is a person. Prepare a list of questions. Tell the person why you are doing a presentation. Ask for permission to quote his or her words. Maybe you can even make a video and use it in your presentation.

Once you have found a source, the next step is to take notes. Search your sources for the answers to the questions on your KWHL chart. You can use note cards or a notebook to take notes. You can also use a computer to type your notes. The key is to stay organized.

The diagram on the next page shows you one way to take notes. However you decide to take notes, you will want to keep track of certain pieces of information.

Most of the time, you should write notes in your own words. But sometimes you will find whole sentences that are tough to change. If this happens, put quotation marks around anything that you copy word for word into your notes. Quotation marks remind you to tell your audience that the words belong to somebody else. Quotations are especially helpful when you are talking about another person's opinion. When this happens, make sure your audience understands that you are presenting an opinion, not a fact.

Your notes should be brief. Except for direct quotes, you don't have to write out everything the author says. Don't worry about writing your notes in complete sentences, either. What's important is that you can understand what you wrote when you use it later.

Keep track of all your sources as you take notes. You will have to give credit to the sources of your presentation. At the end of your presentation you will include a bibliography. This is an alphabetical list of all the sources you used for your research. Ask your teacher or librarian for help with writing a bibliography.

Example: Notes with Source Information

Your notes will help you write an organized presentation.

3

Draft and Revise

You have chosen and explored your topic, and you have found lots of amazing facts. Now you're ready for **Step 3: Draft and revise**. First, organize your information. Your notes will fit into different categories. These will become the sections of your presentation.

Your talk should not have too many sections. Three is a good choice. Expert Malcolm Kushner says, "A grouping of three items makes a powerful impression on the human mind."[4]

Put your note cards into different categories. For an ostrich presentation, your first category might be "what ostriches eat." Your next category of notes might be

Step 1: Choose Your Topic

Step 2: Explore Your Topic

Step 3: Draft and Revise

Step 4: Add Visual Aids

Step 5: Rehearse and Present

Step 6: Review and Publish

21

Outline in Problem-Solution Order

Problem: How to be more Earth-Friendly

Main idea: Recycle at home and school (Solution 1)
Supporting detail: What items can be recycled
Supporting detail: How to set up recycling bins
Supporting detail: Recycling tips

Main idea: Use less water (Solution 2)
Supporting detail: Turn off water while brushing teeth
Supporting detail: Tell your family to fix drippy faucets
Supporting detail: Take shorter showers

Main idea: Make nature-friendly choices (Solution 3)
Supporting detail: Plant a tree
Supporting detail: Walk or ride bikes to save gas
Supporting detail: Cut six-pack plastic rings so they don't choke animals

"where ostriches live." As you sort your note cards, you will find that some information doesn't fit—or you might have too much! Leave out items that don't belong in your three main sections. Keep information that will grab your audience's attention.

Once you have decided on your sections, you need to create a writing plan. An outline is a popular type of writing plan. It is a numbered list of all of your main ideas and supporting details in order. You can write your plan in your notebook or type it on a computer.

Decide on an order for the sections of your presentation. What order would make it easiest for the audience to follow what you say? Chronological order is often a good choice. This means you talk about events in the same order they happened. Another option is to start by describing a problem, and then listing a few solutions.

Once your writing plan is ready, you can begin drafting. A draft is one try at writing something. While you draft, remember that good presentations have a beginning, a middle, and an ending.

The introduction, or beginning, has many purposes. First, you'll introduce yourself and your topic. After that, try to grab your audience's attention with an interesting question or even a joke. Educator Wendy Rubinyi suggests talking with your audience to get them involved. Can you begin with an audience trivia challenge? Is there a short game you could have audience members play?[5]

The body, or middle, of your presentation is based on your outline. It has each main idea followed by your supporting details. As you draft, keep in mind how long your presentation is supposed to be. Read your draft aloud to figure out how long it will take to present it.

The conclusion, or ending, of your presentation is your last chance to connect with your audience. Sum up your main points. Give your listeners something to remember.

Use transitions to move between sections of your talk. Connecting words like *then*, *next*, *second*, and *finally* will link the sections together smoothly. Connecting words get your audience ready for something new.

Your draft will help you plan what to say in your presentation. You should also make notes about where you'll use a poster, a map, or a prop. You can also include notes about when to use sound or music clips, or where to act out an important event.

Once you have a finished draft, start revising. As you revise, think about how you can make your presentation sound like you as a person. Do you have a personal story that fits the topic? Can you make your words more exciting and specific?

Then decide how you will present the information. Will you memorize what you are going to say? This may be a good idea if you are doing a dramatic reading of a poem or a speech. You can also read your presentation word for word. However, writer Steven Otfinoski doesn't like this choice. If you're reading the whole time, it will be harder to make eye contact with your audience. It will be difficult to use visual aids and technology. And reading something word for word can be boring![6]

A better choice is to use note cards. Each card lists a few keywords from each section of your talk. By following the cards, you remember what to say next. This method allows you to make eye contact with your audience.

number your cards to keep them in order

3

Saving water

1. While brushing teeth · · · · · · · big writing

2. Fix drippy faucets

· · · · · · · · leave space between lines

3. Shorter showers

Here is one exception! If you are quoting someone else during your presentation, write out the quotation word for word so you get it right. Also write down the source of the quotation, so you can tell the audience.

Don't Be a Thief!

Here is one of the most important rules of writing and presenting: Never steal someone else's work! Breaking this rule is called plagiarism. To avoid this major mistake, you can do one of two things. The first option is to rewrite an author's information in your own words. The second option is to quote the original writer directly. In this case, you need to tell the audience who you're quoting. We're not just talking about words, though. This rule is also about pictures, songs, and videos. Remember: If you didn't do the work, someone else did! Always give them credit.

Visual aids like this chart will make your presentation more powerful.

Show and Tell: Visual Aids and Multimedia

You know what you are going to say in your presentation. Now it's time to make the final plans for what you are going to *show*. This is **Step 4: Add visual aids**.

Are there props you can use? If you are teaching the audience to juggle, for example, use some oranges or balls to show them how. First, get permission to use your props at school. Your school might have rules against bringing in cell phones, skateboards, food, or objects with sharp edges. Also, check with the person who is lending you the props. (Don't take your mom's Japanese vase without her permission!) And don't

| Step 1: Choose Your Topic |
| Step 2: Explore Your Topic |
| Step 3: Draft and Revise |
| Step 4: Add Visual Aids |
| Step 5: Rehearse and Present |
| Step 6: Review and Publish |

27

forget to plan how you will get your props to the presentation. Can you carry them on the school bus, or will you need a ride that day?

How about wearing a costume? A complicated costume can be distracting. But if your presentation is about skateboarding safety, it would make sense to wear your helmet and pads.

What kinds of visual aids will help your audience as you make your presentation? If you are talking about westward expansion in the United States, you might show a map of the Lewis and Clark expedition. If you are doing a book report, you could create a chart or poster. Or try using the chalkboard, just like a teacher.

Book Report

Title: Charlotte's Web
Author: E. B. White

Important Characters:

Fern   Wilbur   Charlotte   Templeton

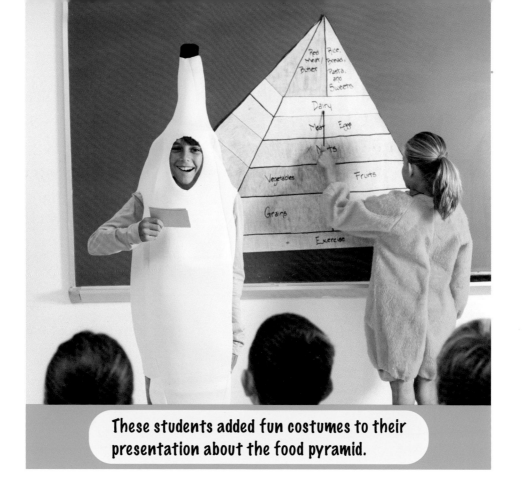

These students added fun costumes to their presentation about the food pyramid.

Choose one main idea for each visual aid. Clear and simple is best. Too much information might confuse your audience. For example, if you're talking about two different types of eagles, make two different visual aids.

Sometimes you will have the exciting option of creating a multimedia presentation. Several computer programs can help you do this. One of the most popular is Microsoft® PowerPoint. These programs allow you to use photographs and videos in your presentation. Writer Geetesh Bajaj points out that you can play MP3 audio files within PowerPoint.[7] (If you do this, read the sidebar "Don't Be a Thief" on page 25 first.)

Your goal is to create a slideshow that helps present your information. Many presenters use bullet points to organize the information on each slide. Look at the student model below. Each bullet point has one important detail.

Multimedia Slide Show

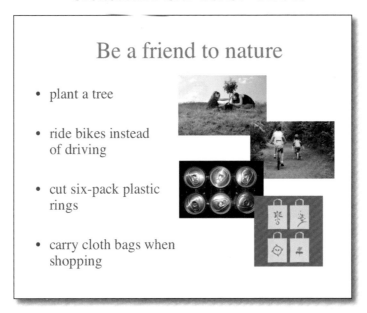

Writer Cliff Atkinson says that your slides need to go beyond bullet points, though. Multimedia presentations need to tell a story.[8] They need a beginning, a middle, and an end.

It is easy to go overboard with technology. Don't use lots of animation and tons of bright colors to impress your audience. Too many tricks can be distracting. The model below shows you what can happen when you play around with a slide too much.

Badly Designed Multimedia Slide

Here are some guidelines to follow when you are creating slides (notice the use of bullet points):

- Don't put too much information on one slide. Three or four lines of text is plenty.

- Limit the number of fonts to one or two.

- Choose fonts that are 18 points or larger so they are easy to read.

- Use a simple background.

- Choose just a few colors, perhaps three or four.

- Proofread your slides!

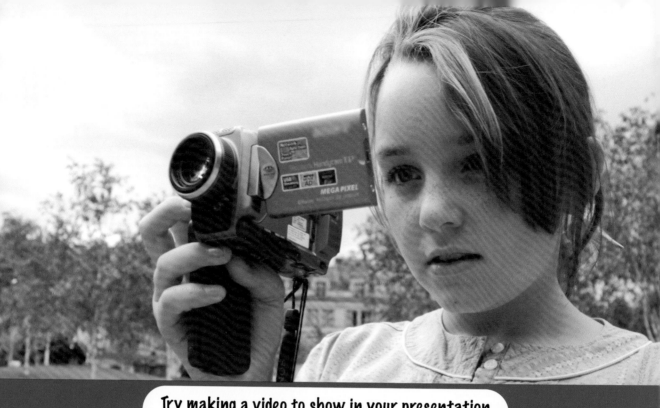

Try making a video to show in your presentation. Your audience will enjoy this visual aid.

Educator Wendy Rubinyi suggests that you print out copies of your slides to use as your presentation note cards. Just remember not to read directly from the slides.[9] Use the slides as reminders to explain more about your topic. Your technology shouldn't do your presentation for you.

Consider some other forms of technology. For a talk about soccer, you could create a video showing different types of kicks. If your report is on Mexico, you can play a CD of some Mexican music. Again, just remember to choose technology that adds to your presentation instead of taking it over.

Take the Stage

We've reached **Step 5: Rehearse and present!** First, give yourself a day to practice your presentation alone, in front of a mirror. Get familiar with your note cards. Remember not to read the cards word for word. They are just a reminder of what you want to say.

Listen to yourself carefully. Does your presentation make sense? Is it easy to follow? Are you using correct grammar and appropriate language for your audience? Are there any words you can't pronounce? Are there any tongue twisters? Practice until your presentation is as strong as possible.

Step 1: Choose Your Topic

Step 2: Explore Your Topic

Step 3: Draft and Revise

Step 4: Add Visual Aids

Step 5: Rehearse and Present

Step 6: Review and Publish

Now it's time to invite a relative or a friend to be your test audience. This gives you a chance to make final changes. Practice using your visual aids and technology. If your teacher gave you a rubric, show it to your test audience. A rubric is a list of your assignment's requirements. Since your teacher uses it to grade your work, your test audience should use it, too.

As you rehearse, check your timing. Keep in mind that it usually takes a little longer to give a presentation in front of a real audience. Then prepare a "to-do" checklist like the one on the next page so you are all ready for the big day.

Suddenly the big day will be here! You've worked hard to prepare and practice. But you might have one little problem. You're nervous! Butterflies seem to be staging a battle in your stomach. There is good news, though. Communication expert Malcolm Kushner says that a few jitters can actually help you do a better job. It's like a ball player getting pumped up for a big game.[10]

Other times, the nerves take over. This is called stage fright. People with stage fright feel like they can't get up in front of an audience. But don't let stage fright stop you. Once you begin talking, you will find it is easier than you thought. Most people find that presenting is a lot of fun!

There are several things you can do if you feel nervous. You have already done one of the most important things. You have taken plenty of time to prepare and practice. That will make a big difference when you are standing in front of an audience.

[Copy onto a separate piece of paper.]

To-do Checklist for Presentation Day

Before School
- ☐ wear my special outfit
- ☐ eat breakfast
- ☐ brush hair and teeth
- ☐ bring notes and visual aids to school

Before Presentation
- ☐ get a drink
- ☐ visit restroom
- ☐ make sure note cards are in order
- ☐ prepare computer (or other technology)

During Presentation
- ☐ take a deep breath and smile!
- ☐ find a friendly face

End of Presentation
- ☐ thank the audience
- ☐ smile and accept applause
- ☐ answer audience questions

Don't focus on being afraid. Instead, imagine yourself feeling confident and proud. Imagine everybody applauding because you've done so well. Remember to show the audience how excited you are about your topic. They will become excited too. This will help you feel sure of yourself.

Steven Otfinoski says that moving around will make your talk more interesting. Make hand gestures when you say something important. Point at a visual aid or write on the board.[11]

Finally, remember to breathe! Take a good, deep breath. That will help you relax.

If you are using a slideshow, talk to your audience, not the computer. Make sure not to rush. Give your listeners enough time to look at each slide.

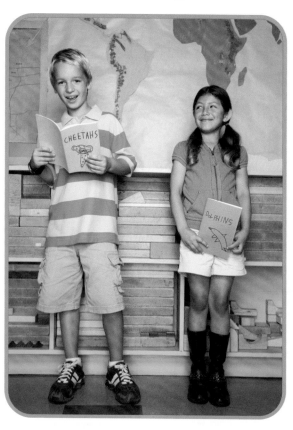

Dress for Success

Looking your best will help you feel more confident. You don't have to wear a suit or a fancy dress. Just make sure your clothes are clean and comfortable. They should fit in with what your school or group allows. Avoid wearing T-shirts with funny sayings. Take off that jingly jewelry! You don't want to distract the audience.

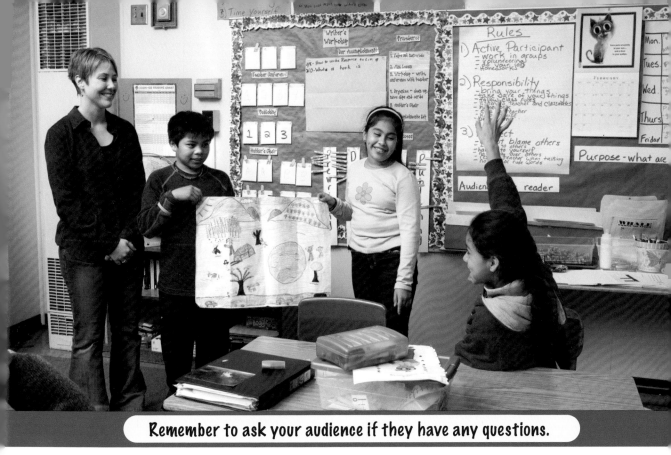

Remember to ask your audience if they have any questions.

Think about how you are using your voice. Speak clearly. Don't rush! Nerves can make you talk too fast. Avoid "filler" words or sounds such as "like" or "um." Make sure you are talking loudly enough for the audience to hear you.

When you have finished speaking, ask if your audience has any questions. If you don't know every answer, that's okay. Just tell the audience member, "That's a great question, but I don't know the answer."

Finally, thank the audience for listening—and wait for the applause!

A student makes a presentation at a school assembly.

6

After the Applause

Whew! Your presentation is finished. Thanks to all of your hard work, it probably went even better than you hoped. Now, there is one last step to take. This is **Step 6: Review and publish**. Evaluate yourself. What makes you proud of your performance? What were your main challenges? How will you improve for next time?

Reflect on how you did at each stage of preparation and performance. You might want to write your thoughts in a notebook or on the computer. It also helps to sit down with a partner or group to talk through your presentation. The key is to do

Step 1: Choose Your Topic

Step 2: Explore Your Topic

Step 3: Draft and Revise

Step 4: Add Visual Aids

Step 5: Rehearse and Present

Step 6: Review and Publish

it soon after your presentation. Otherwise you'll forget all the details.

[Copy onto a separate piece of paper.]

Self Review

Reflect on the job you did, and then answer these questions. Your goal is to give an even better presentation next time.

- What did you do well?

- What were your challenges?

- What did you learn?

- What would you do differently for your next presentation?

- Did you spend enough time gathering and organizing your information? Explain.

- Did you spend enough time practicing? Explain.

- If you used visual aids or technology, how did it go?

- If you were nervous, what helped you get over it?

During your presentation, you might have noticed that the audience can make a big difference. Was your audience full of good listeners? Did they nod when you made good points? Did they laugh at your jokes? Did they ask interesting questions? Those are the signs of an attentive audience.

You can also work on skills that will make you a better audience member for other presenters. Pay careful attention. Keep your eyes on the speaker instead of staring out the window. Keep your notebook open so you can jot down notes or questions. Only ask questions that relate to the speaker's topic.

Another helpful step is doing a peer review with a classmate. It isn't always easy to give feedback. Some people focus only on the things that went wrong. If you do this, you might upset your classmate. Other people give feedback that is too general. For example, they say that everything was "great," even when it wasn't. This feedback doesn't give the presenter any ideas for how to improve.

A peer review will help you review your performance and do better next time.

[Copy onto a separate piece of paper.]

Peer Review Form

Answer the following questions.

- Did the presentation have a clear beginning, middle, and end?

- Did the presentation have lots of descriptive details?

- What was the most interesting thing you learned?

- Did the presenter speak loudly and clearly?

- Did the presenter make eye contact with the audience?

- How were the visual aids and props?

- If you saw a slideshow, were the slides easy to follow?

- List three things you really liked.

- List two things you would change.

It is best to offer both positive and constructive feedback. Start with something positive. Then think about what you can say that is honest but still kind and helpful. Writer Garth Sundem suggests that you "offer three compliments before adding two ideas for improvement."[12]

It also helps to look at the rubric from your teacher. How well did your classmate follow the guidelines?

Organize your thoughts by using the rubric as well as the peer review form on the previous page.

If you receive feedback for your presentation, consider it carefully. What did people enjoy the most? What do you need to work on? If you could give this presentation again, what changes would you make?

You worked so hard. Your presentation was over so fast! How can you make the presentation useful to even more people? You find a way to publish it.

Perhaps you could make a video of your presentation. Then you could send the video to your local cable television station. Does your town have a talent show or a speaking competition where you could perform your poem? Maybe you could read your piece at a school assembly or over the loudspeaker. Perhaps you could perform at a nursing home, your brother's preschool, or for your scout troop. Remember that if you have used other people's work in your presentation, you may need permission to use it outside of school.

Then look for opportunities to give new presentations. Maybe you can join the drama club, become a member of the student council, or create an exhibit for the science fair. Find a local 4-H club. They can help you develop your public speaking skills.

One thing is sure. The more exercise you give your presentation "muscles," the stronger they will become!

Glossary

accurate—Correct; without mistakes.

animation—A visual effect that makes art or text move.

audience—People who are watching or listening to something.

bibliography—A list of all the sources used in a report or presentation.

brainstorming—Coming up with as many ideas as possible.

bullet points—Dots or symbols that set off each item in a list.

chronological order—The order of events as they actually happen, one after the other.

constructive—Helpful, such as feedback that gives specific ideas for improvement.

dramatic reading—A presentation of a piece of writing. The reader uses entertaining voices and shows the emotions of the writing.

graphic organizers—Visual tools that help put information in order.

impression—A lasting impact or effect.

interview—A conversation with a person to find out valuable information.

keywords—Words that relate to a certain topic. They help you find information about a topic on the Internet or in a library catalog.

multimedia—Involving a mix of different media such as video, sound, animation, and illustrations.

outline—A numbered list of the ideas that will be in a report.

peer review—The process of giving feedback to someone in your class or group.

persuasive—Able to make someone believe or agree with something.

pivotal—Very important.

plagiarism—Using someone else's work without giving them credit, as if it were your own.

presentation—A talk or speech providing information or ideas, often including visual aids and multimedia technology.

prewriting—Getting organized before you write.

props—Items used to demonstrate something, such as an umbrella used to show how to stay dry in the rain.

publish—To put a work of writing or art in final form and present it to the public.

quote—To repeat the exact words that somebody else said or wrote.

reference materials—Books, encyclopedias, Web sites, or other sources that contain basic information.

research—The process of finding information about a topic.

rubric—A guide that shows how your work will be evaluated.

slides—The individual pages of a multimedia presentation.

sources—Things that give you information, such as books, magazines, Web sites, and people.

technology—Machines or other tools that help people complete a task. For a presentation, common technology includes computers, video cameras, and CD players.

visual aids—Physical objects with pictures that help explain information, such as maps, photographs, props, and charts.

Further Reading

Books

Gaines, Ann Graham. *Ace Your Internet Research.* Berkeley Heights, N.J.:
    Enslow Publishers, 2009.

Ryan, Margaret. *Extraordinary Oral Presentations.* New York: Franklin
    Watts, 2006.

Thornhill, Samantha. *Everybody Hates School Presentations.* New York:
    Simon Spotlight, 2008.

On the Internet

Create a PowerPoint presentation.
    http://learning.loc.gov/learn/educators/workshop/pizazz/

Get ideas for putting on a play with your classmates.
    http://pbskids.org/zoom/activities/playhouse/

You can improve your presentation skills by joining 4-H and other groups!
    http://www.4-h.org/

Chapter Notes

1. Personal interview with Wendy Rubinyi, February 19, 2008.

2. Alex Barnett, *Words That Changed America: Great Speeches That Inspired, Challenged, Healed, and Enlightened* (New York: Lyons Press, 2003), p. VIII.

3. Sara Holbrook, *Wham! It's a Poetry Jam: Discovering Performance Poetry* (Honesdale, Pa.: Boyds Mills Press, 2002), p. 28.

4. Malcolm Kushner, *Public Speaking for Dummies*, 2nd Edition (Hoboken, N.J.: Wiley Publishing, 2004), p. 99.

5. Personal interview with Wendy Rubinyi, February 19, 2008.

6. Steven Otfinoski, *Speaking Up, Speaking Out: A Kid's Guide to Making Speeches, Oral Reports, and Conversation* (Brookfield, Conn.: The Millbrook Press, 1996), p. 47.

7. Geetesh Bajaj, *Cutting Edge PowerPoint 2007 for Dummies* (Hoboken, N.J.: Wiley Publishing, 2007), p. 230.

8. Cliff Atkinson, "The First Five Slides: Unlocking the Story Buried in Your Presentation," March 2005, <http://www.sociablemedia.com/articles_first_five.htm> (February 21, 2008).

9. Personal interview with Wendy Rubinyi, February 19, 2008.

10. Kushner, p. 127.

11. Otfinoski, p. 39.

12. Garth Sundem, M. M., *Improving Student Writing Skills* (Huntington Beach, Calif.: Shell Educational Publishing, 2006), p. 32.

Index